EATING AND DRINKING ON THE OPEN ROAD

"...an opinionated little compendium."
~ New York Times

"...irresistible little guide."
~ Chicago Tribune

"an elegant, small guide..."
~ Minneapolis Star Tribune

""...a terrific primer for first-time visitors."
~ Houston Chronicle

""...opening up the world of good eating with their innovative paperback series."
~ Salt Lake Tribune

"...travelers who know their cervelle *(brains) from* cervelle de canut *(herbed cheese spread)."*
~ USA Today

**OPEN ROAD TRAVEL GUIDES – YOUR GUIDES
TO PLANET EARTH!**

Whether you're going abroad or planning a trip to the United States, take Open Road along on your journey. Our books have been praised by **Travel & Leisure**, **The Los Angeles Times**, **Newsday**, **Booklist**, **US News & World Report**, **Endless Vacation**, **American Bookseller**, **Coast to Coast** and many other magazines and newspapers!

Don't just see the world - experience it with Open Road!

ABOUT THE AUTHORS

Michael Dillon is a graphic designer. Andy Herbach is a lawyer. Both authors reside in Milwaukee, Wisconsin. They are the authors of *Eating and Drinking in Paris*, *Eating and Drinking in Italy*, *Eating and Drinking in Spain* **and** *Eating and Drinking in Latin America*.

You can e-mail comments, additions and corrections through www.eatndrink.com.

OPEN ROAD –
TRAVEL GUIDES TO PLANET EARTH!

Open Road Publishing has guide books to exciting, fun destinations on four continents. As veteran travelers, our goal is to bring you the best travel guides available anywhere!

No small task, but here's what we offer:

- All Open Road travel guides are written by authors with a distinct, opinionated point of view – not some sterile committee or team of writers. Our authors are experts in the areas covered and are polished writers.

- Our guides are geared to people who want to make their own travel choices. We'll show you how to discover the real destination – not just see some place from a tour bus window.

- We're strong on the basics, but we also provide terrific choices for those looking to get off the beaten path and experience the country or city – not just see it or pass through it.

- We give you the best, but we also tell you about the worst and what to avoid. Nobody should waste his or her time and money on their hard-earned vacation because of bad or inadequate travel advice.

- Our guides assume nothing. We tell you everything you need to know to have the trip of a lifetime – presented in a fun, literate, no-nonsense style.

- And, above all, we welcome your input, ideas, and suggestions to help us put out the best travel guides possible..

EATING AND DRINKING IN

Italy

•

Italian Menu Reader and Restaurant Guide

Andy Herbach and Michael Dillon

OPEN ROAD PUBLISHING

Third Edition

Copyright © 2004 by Andy Herbach and Michael Dillon
- All Rights Reserved -

Cover design and illustration by Michael Dillon
Back cover photo by Elizabeth Enslen Dillon

Library of Congress Control No. 2004105641
ISBN 1-59360-018-6

Table of Contents

Introduction

Can you imagine a foreign traveler who speaks basic English understanding what prime rib is? Or a porterhouse? Veggie platter, anyone? Buffalo wings? Sloppy Joes?

Even people who speak passable Italian can have trouble reading a menu. You may know *ricotta* cheese, but not *malfatti di ricotta* which means "badly made," a reference to the handmade dumpling with *ricotta* cheese filling. You may be surprised to find *puttanesca* (which means *in the style of a prostitute*) on the menu. It is a sauce of tomatoes, capers, black olives and garlic.

Understanding the customs and food of a country helps travelers understand the people who live in the country.

If you love to travel as we do, you know the importance of a good guide. The same is true of dining. A good guide can make all the difference between a memorable evening and a dizzyingly bad one. This guide will help you find your way around a menu written in Italian. It gives you the freedom to enter places you might never have before and order a dinner without shouting, pointing and hand waving. Instead of fumbling with a bulky, conspicuous tourist guide (most of which usually include a very incomplete listing of foods) in a restaurant, this book is a pocket-sized alphabetical listing of food and drink commonly found on menus in Italy.

Although, now that we think about it, a dinner without shouting and hand waving is not truly Italian.

6

Of course, traveling to a foreign country means something different to everyone. For every vacation there are different expectations, different needs, and every traveler has his or her own idea of what will make that vacation memorable. For us, the making of a memorable vacation begins and ends with food.

We spent the morning staring at the Sistine Chapel and the Vatican Museum, but what stands out in our minds is the wonderful lunch in the *trattoria* afterward. Although the waiter was less than helpful (in fact, not helpful at all), the creamy shrimp pasta dish was as heavenly as Michelangelo's masterpiece. We spent a morning driving to see the Leaning Tower of Pisa, but the grilled lamb in Lerici made the day.

We know the panic of opening a menu without recognizing one word on it and the disappointment of being served something other than what you thought you'd ordered. On our first trip to Europe, we were served a plate of cold brains; we thought we had ordered chicken. This guide was created for the traveler who wants to enjoy, appreciate and experience authentic cuisine *and* know what he or she is eating.

The next time you find yourself seated in a red-tiled courtyard with the scent of simmering garlic in the night air and an incomprehensible menu in your hands, simply pull this guide from your pocket and get ready to enjoy the delicious cuisine of Italy.

In Italy and Ticino (the Italian-speaking region of Switzerland), the menu is almost always posted outside of the restaurant or in a window. This makes choosing a restaurant easy and fun as you "window shop" for your next meal.

Remember that the dish that you ordered may not be exactly as described in this guide. Every chef is (and should be) innovative. What we have listed for you in this guide is the most common version of a dish.

If a menu has an English translation it does not mean that the translation is correct.

In Italy, it is customary to order a first course (pasta, rice or soup), a second course (meat, poultry or fish) and a side dish (salad, potato or vegetable). Rarely does an Italian order only a first course (such as ordering only pasta), but that doesn't mean you have to.

Tipping

A 10% to 15% service charge is almost always added to your bill (*il conto*) in Italy. Depending on the service, it is customary to leave an additional 5% to 10%. The menu will usually note that service is included (*servizio incluso* or *servizio compreso*). A service charge, by law, is included in all restaurant bills in Ticino.

You will often find *coperto* or cover charge on your menu (a small charge just for placing your butt at the table).

Mealtimes

In northern Italy, lunch is served from noon to around 2 p.m., and dinner from 7 p.m. to 10 p.m. In the south, lunch is served from 1 p.m. and dinner from 8 p.m. No "early bird special" in Italy. Ticino's hours are the same as in northern Italy.

8

Water

Europeans joke that you can tell a U.S. tourist from his fanny pack, clothes and ubiquitous bottle of mineral water. Tap water is safe in Italy and Switzerland. Occasionally, you will find *non potabile* signs in restrooms (especially in the rest stops of highways). This means that the water is not safe for drinking.

Waiters and waitresses will often bring *acqua minerale* (mineral water) to your table. You will be charged for it, so if you do not want mineral water ask for *acqua semplice* or *acqua di rubinetto* (tap water).

"Acqua di Rubinetto" is safe to drink but can taste weird. We usually order bottled water with meals.

 RESTAURANTS IN THIS GUIDE

Each of our recommended restaurants offers something different. Some have great food and little ambiance. Others have great ambiance and adequate food. Still others have both. Our goal is to find restaurants that are moderately priced and enjoyable. All restaurants have been tried and tested. Not enough can be said for a friendly welcome and great service. No matter how fabulous the meal, the experience will always be better when the staff treats you as if they actually want you there rather than simply tolerating your presence.

Times can change and restaurants can close, so do a walk-by earlier in the day or the day before, if possible. Our full list of restaurants starting on page 100 includes many of the eating establishments listed below.

Types of Eating Establishments

Bacaro: Venetian wine bar serving snacks like Spanish *tapas*.
Bar: Bars serve espresso, cappuccino, rolls, small sandwiches,

alcoholic beverages and soft drinks.

Bottiglieria: Simple drinking establishments with limited menus but plenty of bottles of wine. Originally, these "bottle shops" served only liquor. Also called *fiaschetteria*, *cantina* or *trani*.

Enoteca: Wine bar.

Gelateria: Shop serving *gelato* (ice cream).

Grotta: Ticino has many *grotte*. These are village restaurants that take their name from caves used to store food and wine. Originally, a *grotta* was a simple eating establishment, but today many are quite expensive with extensive menus.

Locanda: Found in the country, serves regional meats and seafood.

Osteria: A tavern or wine shop. This name has also come to refer to a restaurant. These can also be called *cucina* or *hostaria*.

Paninoteca: Usually serves only sandwiches.

Pasticceria: Pastry shop.

Pizza Rustica: Common in central Italy; serves large rectangular pizzas with thicker crusts and more toppings than usually found in a *pizzeria*. You can order as much as you want, and pay by weight.

Pizzeria: We think you can figure this one out.

Ristorante: A restaurant.

Rosticceria: A deli, sometimes with a few tables, where you can order grilled meats (especially chicken).

Tavola Calda: Small restaurant with take-out or fast foods and usually with a few tables.

Trattoria: Less expensive family-run restaurant, usually not too fancy.

Tips for Budget Dining in Italy

There is no need to spend a lot of money in Italy to eat good food. There are all kinds of fabulous foods to be had inexpensively all over Italy.

Eat at a neighborhood restaurant or *trattoria*. You'll always know the price of a meal before entering, as almost all restaurants in Italy post the menu and prices in the window. Never order anything whose price is not known in advance. For instance, if you see *etto* on a menu in Venice this means that you are paying by weight (an *etto* is 100 grams), which can be extremely expensive.

Delis and food stores can provide cheap and wonderful meals. Buy cheese, bread, wine and other snacks and have a picnic. Remember to pack a corkscrew and eating utensils when you leave home.

Lunch, even at the most expensive restaurants listed in this guide, always has a lower price. So, have lunch as your main meal.

Restaurants that have menus written in English (especially those near tourist attractions) are almost always more expensive than neighborhood restaurants.

Street vendors generally sell inexpensive and good food. For the cost of a cup of coffee or a drink, you can linger at a café and watch the world pass you by for as long as you want. It's one of Italy's greatest bargains.

And don't eat at McDonald's, for God's sake.

OUR MISSION

As silly as it might sound, we have one:

No Menus in English.

Aside from, say, in England.

We want people to eat in restaurants that don't provide English menus. We don't like to see the United States when we're visiting Italy; we want foreign when we're on foreign soil. When we visited Athens we were horrified to see a gigantic neon-and-plastic, two-story Kenny Rogers Roast Chicken franchise on Syntagma Square right smack across from the Greek Parliament. On the beautiful port of Marigot on the island of St. Martin in the French West Indies, a single Kentucky Fried Chicken put all of the small, locally owned and picturesque grill shacks, called *lolos*, out of business, virtually destroying what was charming about the port. We have nothing against fast food, but when we're in Italy, we want it to look Italian. We don't want to see the golden arches near the Leaning Tower and we don't want to see a menu in English. As we see it, a menu in English is the first step in the Americanization of the restaurants of the world, the first domino. And once it's not foreign, what's the point of going?

⚛ ITALY ⚛

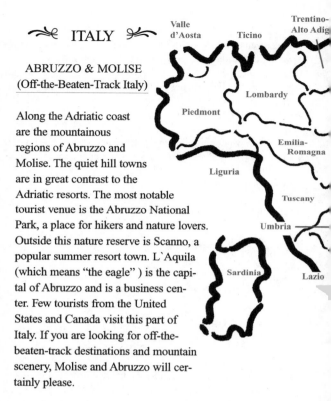

ABRUZZO & MOLISE
(Off-the-Beaten-Track Italy)

Along the Adriatic coast are the mountainous regions of Abruzzo and Molise. The quiet hill towns are in great contrast to the Adriatic resorts. The most notable tourist venue is the Abruzzo National Park, a place for hikers and nature lovers. Outside this nature reserve is Scanno, a popular summer resort town. L`Aquila (which means "the eagle") is the capital of Abruzzo and is a business center. Few tourists from the United States and Canada visit this part of Italy. If you are looking for off-the-beaten-track destinations and mountain scenery, Molise and Abruzzo will certainly please.

Inland, you will find menus dominated by *capretto* (baby goat), *agnello arrosto* (roast lamb), and *porchetta* (roast pig). On the coast (in restaurants not serving tourist fare) try *brodetto* (fish soup). *Centerbe* (a green herb liquor) accompanies many meals. For dessert, try *confetti* (flower-shaped candy made from sugar-coated almonds).

APULIA (The "Heel" of Italy)

Apulia (Puglia) is the "heel" of Italy. Oppressively hot in July and August, a rainy day is rare. Apulia is a large wine-producing region. The area is not frequented by many North American tourists. The baroque town of Martina Franca and the white-washed town of Locorotondo are in the wine region and worth a visit. Part of the coast is heavily industrialized with immense steelworks. Bari is a modern port and a common departure point for travelers to Greece. *Trulli*, dome-shaped whitewashed stone buildings, are indigenous to the area. The largest collection of *trulli*, can be found near Alberobello. The Adriatic fishing ports have architecture similar to the old Venetian ports. Taranto is a modern town as is the important port of Brindisi, another frequent departure point for visits to Greece. Not to be missed is the lovely Baroque town of Lecce.

Focaccia barese (stuffed pizza), often with *burrata* (very buttery cheese), *triglia* (red mullet), *spigola* (sea bass), *orecchiette con le cime di rapa* (ear-shaped pasta with turnips) and *tiella di riso e cozze* (a mussels, rice and potato dish) can all be found on Apulia's menus. Some avoid the *polpi arricciati* ("curled octopus") when they see that the octopus is beaten and twirled in a basket in order to get the desired "curled" shape of the octopus. *Bianco di Martina* is a common fortified wine found in Apulia.

BASILICATA (Undiscovered Italy)

This area was once known as Lucania. One of Italy's smallest regions, Basilicata is also its poorest. Mountainous and barren, Basilicata is not visited by many tourists. The capital city of Potenza was badly damaged in a 1980's earthquake. The hill town of Maratea is dramatically situated on the coast. Here, in small villages such as Metaponto and Matera, you experience the simple Italy.

The spicy *sugna piccante* (pork sauce) flavors many dishes. *Maiale* (pork) is found on most menus, and cured meats like

13

the sausage *luganega*, *luganica* or *lucanica* (there are even more spellings than this!) are common. *Peperoncini* (small hot green peppers preserved in oil) are added to many dishes. Try *scamorza* cheese (the local version of aged *mozzarella*).

CALABRIA (The "Toe" of Italy)

Sun, white-sand beaches, rugged mountains, olive groves and the huge rock of Scilla are all found on the "toe" of Italy. The area was once known as Magna Graecia, and there are villages where a Greek dialect is still spoken. The mountain towns such as Serra San Bruno remain as they were several hundred years ago. Rossano is a beautiful medieval town overlooking a great ravine. Consenza is a town built on a steep hillside with an interesting (almost dilapidated) look to it. Many tourists find themselves in modern Reggio on their way to Sicily. The small towns of Pizzo and Tropea are worth a visit to experience the true Calabria. We would be remiss if we did not mention that some areas of Calabria are strongholds of the local mafia and not recommended for travel.

Costolette d'agnello (lamb chops) and *pesce spada* (swordfish) are found on most menus. *Novellame* is a spread of salted anchovies and *peperoncino* sauce. Pasta is often served with chickpeas (*ceci*). *Stracotto* is a beef stew which in Calabria includes carrots, mushrooms, onions, nutmeg and cloves. *Caviale del sud* or "caviar of the south" is a dish of fried fish preserved in oil and powdered with *peperoncino*. *Fichi* (figs) are featured in many desserts.

CAMPANIA (Naples, Capri & the Amalfi Coast)

Naples, in the shadow of Vesuvius, is congested, noisy, has a reputation as dangerous, and is not an easy city for the tourist. After a quick view of Naples' old town along the harbor, most head for the nearby ruins of Herculaneum and Pompeii. It is an eerie experience walking through nearly perfectly preserved ancient communities buried by the volcanic eruption of

Vesuvius. The volcanic island of Ischia and nearby Capri are often overrun by day trippers in high season.

Although it can be expensive, Capri (with its breathtaking vistas) remains the favorite of many returning visitors. The gateway to the Amalfi coast is Sorrento, perched over the sea. The Amalfi coast is the most spectacular coastal drive in Italy (if you have the nerve to drive it in high season). Positano has a great beach with a view of the town perched on the bluff. Amalfi and Ravello, further down the Amalfi coast, have spectacular views. The Amalfi coast reigns as one of the most scenic and photographed coasts in the world.

Along the coast, seafood is prevalent, especially *polpi affogati* (octopus in a spicy tomato sauce). Pizza, said to have originated in Naples, is found in many varieties. *Pizza alla Napoletana* is pizza with tomato sauce and anchovies. You will eat tomatoes here like you have never had before. Many pasta dishes are served *al pomodoro* (with a tomato sauce). Meat is often cooked *alla pizzaiola* (in a tomato sauce with garlic). *Partenopea* on a menu simply means served Naples style. For dessert try *sfogliatella* (flaky pastry filled with sweet *ricotta* cheese).

EMILIA-ROMAGNA (From the Adriatic Sea to Central Italy)

The Romans built a grand road from Rimini on the Adriatic Sea to Piacenza in central Italy. The towns that now make up this region developed along this road, the Via Emilia. Piacenza is a major industrial city with a lovely downtown. Parma (which lends its name to the famous Parma ham or *prosciutto*), Modena (home to the Ferrari and Maserati automobiles), Bologna (a learning center, important city for commerce, and *the* food town in Italy), and Ferrara (less spoiled by modern times than the others) are all towns with important historic centers. Imposing Ravenna is in contrast to the most popular Adriatic resort of Rimini. Be careful, as Rimini can be quite dull, even completely closed, off season and extremely overcrowded in season.

The coast features *brodetto* (fish soup). *Prosciutto di Parma* (Parma ham) is common as is *risotto* (the famous Italian rice dish). Suckling pig is called *lattonzolo* here. For dessert, try *castagnole* (chestnut fritters). True Italian food is rare in Rimini, which has revised its menus to cater to the European package tourist.

FRIULI-VENEZIA GIULIA (Trieste & the Austrian Border)

This region borders on Austria and Slovenia. Udine is the capital but Trieste draws the most attention. Trieste, which remained under United Nations control until 1954, is an interesting mix of Austrian and Italian with a Slavic influence from the former Yugoslav republics. The architecture along the port demonstrates the mix of rulers in Trieste. Our several trips to Trieste have made us realize that this area is often, unfortunately, overlooked by tourists. White wine is produced in the hills of Friuli-Venezia Giulia. Visit the towns of Colli Orientali and Collio. The small mountain towns along the Austrian border allow the visitor to experience a mixture of Italy and Austria.

Jota is a minestrone found here and usually contains sauerkraut. *Polenta* (cornmeal mush) is found everywhere. *Brodetto* (fish soup) is common in the coastal area of this region. *Cialzons* are sweet-and-sour pasta found here. The town of San Daniele is the home of *prosciutto di San Daniele* (a cured ham). The Slavic influence is found in the Trieste dessert of *gubana* (sweet bread roll) and the Austrian influence is found in the many coffeehouses of Trieste.

LAZIO (Rome & its Environs)

Lazio (also called Latium) is the region around Rome. To try to list Rome's main attractions would require another guide. Rome can be a frustrating city (it can be hard to carry on a conversation while walking down the street due to the constant traffic noise). But, difficulties aside, few places in the world have so many important sites in such a small area,

including the Vatican with its Sistine Chapel, Circus Maximus, the Spanish Steps, the Trevi Fountain, the catacombs...

Sperlonga, San Felice Circeo, Santa Severa and Santa Marinella are all coastal towns worth a visit. Ostia is a large coastal city near Rome and was the main Roman port. Its impressive ruins are an easy day trip from Rome. In inland Lazio, you may visit Tivoli (with Hadrian's Villa), Palestrina, the mountain town of Subiaco and the walled town of Viterbo.

Rome is said to have 5,000 restaurants. In Rome, you can eat just about anything. After a grueling day of sightseeing, stop in a small restaurant (*trattoria*), drink some wine and eat a hearty dish of pasta such as one served *all' arrabbiata* (in a spicy tomato and herb sauce) or *alla carbonara* (with bacon, cheese, olive oil and eggs). Meals often start with *bruschetta* (garlic toast) and end with *grappa* (of which we drank a little too much on our first night here). When in Rome...

LE MARCHE (The Apennines Mountain Region)

The Apennines Mountains separate Le Marche from the rest of Central Italy. Ancona, on the Adriatic coast (a common departure point for Venice) is a modern port town. Pilgrims visit the house of the Virgin Mary in Loreto (brought here, according to legend, by angels). Urbino, one of the lesser-known great Renaissance cities, looks much as it did in the fifteenth century. In the Tronto River Valley, scenic Ascoli Piceno is another Le Marche town worth visiting. Most travelers head for the crowded (package tour-filled) coastal towns. These crowded resorts are in great contrast to the sedate hill towns.

Truffles (*tartufi*) are a specialty here and summer peaches (*pesche*) and plums (*susine*) are some of the best fruits you will ever taste. *Vincigrassi* (baked lasagna dish), *olive all'ascolana* (large stuffed olives), *porchetta* (roast suckling pig) and rabbit (*coniglio)* are popular. *Brodetto di pesce* (fish soup) is found along the coast. In Ancona, *brodetto* contains thirteen varieties of fish.

LIGURIA (The Italian Riviera)

Wedged between mountains and the sea, the coastal region of Liguria stretches from the French border to Tuscany and is a popular tourist destination. Genoa, a large industrial city, is also Italy's biggest port. Tourists usually visit only the old, central part of the city. West of Genoa toward the French border are the bright tourist towns of Ventimiglia and Bordighera. San Remo (with its famous casino) is the largest resort. East from Genoa, you will find the resort of Nervi with beautiful parks. Further down the coast are the resort towns of Camogli, Rapallo, Santa Margherita and of course, perhaps the best known and most beautiful Italian port of Portofino. One drawback is the gridlock in and out of Portofino in high season. Sestri Levante makes a good base for exploring the highlight of any trip to Liguria, the Cinque Terre, five beautiful towns, which until recently were accessible only by train or a series of hiking paths. Perched on dramatic cliffs above the sea, you will experience car-free serenity and an Italy of old. Down the coast is Lerici (where we had one of our most memorable meals in an open-air restaurant on the port).

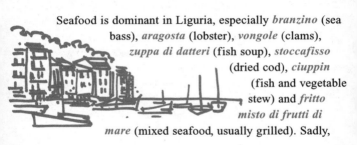

Seafood is dominant in Liguria, especially *branzino* (sea bass), *aragosta* (lobster), *vongole* (clams), *zuppa di datteri* (fish soup), *stoccafisso* (dried cod), *ciuppin* (fish and vegetable stew) and *fritto misto di frutti di mare* (mixed seafood, usually grilled). Sadly, seafood is becoming less common because of pollution and overfishing in the Mediterranean. *Basilico* (basil) grown in the hills above the sea forms the basis of *pesto* and is common in the cuisine of Liguria. Try *ravioli di magro* (pasta stuffed with herbs and *ricotta* cheese).

LOMBARDY (Milan & the Lake District)

Fashionable, modern Milan is an important center of Italian commerce. If you like to shop, Milan is the place. Tourists often visit four important sites: the Duomo (cathedral, especially the ornate roof), La Scala (the opera house), the Last Supper and the Galleria Vittorio Emanuele (the famous glass-domed shopping center).

In great contrast to Milan is the Lake District, including Lakes Orta (often, regrettably, ignored), Maggiore, Como, and Garda. The towns that line these lakes remain dotted with former palaces (many now resorts) with impressive formal gardens. Many believe the Lake District is Italy at its best. On Lake Como, Bellagio is the most famous resort, but Varenna, with its tiny harbor and splendid beach, is the favorite of many.

Trota (trout) is popular in the Lake District. Lombardy specialties include *stracotto* (pot roast), *ossobuco* (braised veal shank) and *capretto* (roast kid). You will find many dishes served *alla milanese* (battered with eggs and breadcrumbs and fried). *Risotto alla milanese* is a popular rice dish with a golden color from the ingredient saffron. *Gorgonzola* (a delicious blue cheese) is often found in pasta dishes. Lombardy cheeses also included *crescenza* (a soft, buttery cheese) and *mascarpone* (a very creamy cheese). *Torrone* (honey and almond nougat) is a common dessert.

19

Sometimes the Alpine regions of Piedmont (which means "foot of the mountain") and Valle d'Aosta (north of Piedmont) feel more like France or Switzerland than Italy. Valle d'Aosta has two official languages: Italian and French. Many come to the largest city in these regions, Turin (Torino), to see the Shroud of Turin (believed by some to be the cloth in which Christ's body was wrapped after the crucifixion). North of Turin, into Valle d'Aosta, is Saint Vincent (a popular gambling resort). Any trip to this area would not be complete without a visit to Breuil-Cervina at the base of the Matterhorn (Monte Cervino) with breathtaking views of this famous mountain peak. Courmayeur, another Alpine resort, is the gateway to Mont Blanc (Monte Bianco) on the French border. The walled city of Aosta is nestled in the Alps. Asti (yes, as in the wine), Novara, Vercelli, and Casale Monferrato are all towns with impressive medieval towers. If you are looking for beautiful mountain scenery, don't miss these regions.

Piemontese on a menu means "Piedmont style" or with white truffles. *Tartufi bianchi* are famous white truffles from Alba and Asti. *Alla Valdostana* on a menu means "Valle d'Aosta style" and usually means with ham and cheese. Roast game, sausages and butter play heavy roles in the local diet. *Tajarin* is thin ribbon pasta made golden with egg yolks. *Fonduta* (fondue) is popular. The French influence can be found in *crespelle* (crêpes). You will find *cervo* (venison), *carbonade* (beef cooked in wine and onions) and *arrosto misto* (grilled meats) here along with *trota* (trout). *Gianduiotti* are hazelnut chocolates found in Turin and one of our favorite treats. *Torta di nocciole*, hazelnut cake, is a must.

SAN MARINO (Europe's Oldest Country)

With about only 25,000 people and 24 square miles, San Marino (totally surrounded by Italy) claims to be Europe's oldest existing country. San Marino's official name is the Most Serene Republic of San Marino, and is located 15 miles inland from the Adriatic Sea resort of Rimini. Its chief industries are tourism and the sale of postage stamps. Mt. Titano, upon which San Marino sits, must be climbed after you leave your car. There are three medieval fortresses on the mountain. The capital, also named San Marino, is a maze of attractive narrow streets.

Food is typical Italian. You'll find *coniglio* (rabbit) and *nidi di rondine* (pasta rolls). Don't miss *caciatella* (San Marino's version of crème caramel).

SARDINIA (SARDEGNA)

The island of Sardinia is located about 115 miles off the western coast of Italy in the Mediterranean. Ten miles to the north is the French island of Corsica. Sardinia has been a part of Italy since 1861. Cagliari, the capital, is on the south coast, which is known for its ancient ruins. For the most part, Sardinia remains unspoiled from its rocky coast to its mountainous interior. The northeastern Costa Smeralda (Emerald Coast) is the only area where tourist development has arrived. Those looking for peace and quiet and even isolation should experience the mountainous inland region of Barbagia.

Lobster (*aragosta*) is plentiful along the coast, and the northern coast of Sardinia is sometimes referred to as the lobster coast. Lamb (*agnello*), rabbit (*cunillu*) and trout (*trota*) are ubiquitous. Grilled meats are a specialty. The shepherds of Sardinia feast on *pane carasau*, which is also known as *carta da musica* (music paper). Durham wheat, salt, water and yeast are the simple ingredients for this wood fire-baked bread. You will find this thin, crispy bread used as a pizza crust.

Other specialties of Sardinia include *porceddu* (roast suckling pig which is the "national" dish of Sardinia), *cascà* (couscous), and many honey-based desserts such as *sebadas* (deep-fried cheese-filled ravioli soaked in honey).

SICILY (SICILIA)

French, Arabs, Spanish and Italians have all controlled Sicily, the largest and most populated island in the Mediterranean. Travelers will find some of the best-preserved Greek and Roman ruins here, along with the ornate architecture of its churches and palaces. Agrigento is home to the most important archaeological site in Sicily, the Greek "Valley of the Temples." Siracusa (Syracuse) is also known for its Greek and Roman ruins. The capital is Palermo, but most travelers head to the medieval town of Taormina on the east coast in the shadows of Mount Etna, an active volcano. Messina (destroyed by both an earthquake and the bombs of World War II) has bland, modern architecture, and is in strong contrast to the picturesque fishing port of Cefalù.

Sicilian cuisine is not simply pasta and olive oil but incorporates Italian, Greek, French, Spanish and Arab influences. Some specialties are *pasta con le sarde* (pasta with fresh sardines), *pesce spada* (swordfish), and the simple *cicina* (a mixture of fried small fish).

Other specialties are *caponata* (sweet-and-sour sauce with eggplant, tomatoes, onions and peppers), *pasta alla Norma* (pasta with a tomato, basil and eggplant sauce topped with *ricotta* cheese) and *costoletta alla siciliana* (thin slices of veal or beef topped with chopped garlic and *parmesan* cheese, then breaded and deep-fried).

Desserts, and Sicilians

are famous for their desserts, include *cannoli* (pastry tubes filled with sweetened *ricotta* cheese) and *cassata alla siciliana* (layered spongecake).

Marsala wine (from the town of the same name) is a fortified wine that can range from rich and sweet to dry.

TICINO (Italian-Speaking Switzerland)

Ticino is the main Italian-speaking canton or region of Switzerland. Palm trees, Italian architecture, Swiss orderliness and Italian food all make Ticino (with its famous resorts of Lugano and Locarno) a great travel destination. Ticino is Switzerland's southernmost canton, bordering on Italy, and has been a part of Switzerland since the early 1800's. This region has always remained strongly Italian. Italian is one of four official languages of Switzerland (along with French, German and Romansh).

Specialties found in Ticino are *risotto ai fiori di zucca* (a rice dish made with a heavy cream base and zucchini flowers stirred in along with *parmesan* cheese), *pancetta arrotolata* (rolled bacon flavored with cloves), *capretto* (baby goat), *fritto misto* (breaded and fried lake fish), *cotto antico* (bay leaf-flavored salami), and *giambonetti di pollo* (stuffed chicken leg). Bread is a staple in all meals, especially bread with a thick crust dusted with flour called *crusca*. Two common cheeses found in Ticino are *formaggini di capra* (fresh goat's-milk cheese) and *formaggini d'Alpe* (a common cow's-milk cheese). Both of these cheeses are eaten with olive oil, salt and pepper.

TRENTINO-ALTO ADIGE (The Dolomites)

The Alto Adige is the far north of Italy and is more like Austria than Italy. The Dolomite Mountains dominate this area. At the Brenner Pass, on the border with Austria, is the town of Bolzano/Bozen (Austrian until 1918). Near Bolzano is the wine town of Caldaro. Bressanone/Brixen is a beautiful mountain town and the Alto Adige's oldest city. Ortisei, San Martino and Madonna di Campiglio are all summer and winter resort towns. Breathtaking views abound in Brunico/Bruneck. Merano has an interesting old town and famous spas. Trento, the capital of Trentino, is more Italian than Austrian and remains an attractive and architecturally interesting town.

Food here is more German than Italian (especially the farther north you travel). Game, dumplings (*knoedel*) and cured ham (*speck*) all stress the German influence. Sauerkraut (*crauti*) is featured heavily in dishes, as are *wurstel* (hot dogs and brats). For dessert, apples, grown in large numbers in the region, are often added to the Germanic dessert of *strudel*.

TUSCANY (One of the World's Most Popular Destinations)

There are so many picturesque towns in Tuscany, space allows only a few highlights. With unspoiled hills, perfectly preserved towns and great food and wine, Tuscany is one of the most popular tourist destinations in Italy and the world. Since childhood, we wanted to see the Leaning Tower of Pisa (and the nearby and lesser-known baptistery). Too bad there are so many hawkers of plastic leaning towers all over Pisa. Siena's main square, the Piazza del Campo, and ornate cathedral are only two gems in the beautiful town with (thankfully) a car-free center. San Gimignano, with its walls and towers, is an incredibly picturesque town. The hilltop towns of Lucca, Montepulciano, Montalcino and Pienza are all worth a visit. Of course, Florence is the favorite of many visitors to Italy. Its wealth of art, housed in buildings which themselves are art, leaves many visitors wanting to return again and again.

Start your meal with *crostini* (toasted bread with various toppings). *La bistecca alla Fiorentina*, a T-bone steak, must not be missed nor should any number of the *pecorino* cheeses. Menus often include dishes served *alla lepre* (in a rabbit-based sauce), *cinghiale* (wild boar), *arista* (roast, seasoned pork loin), and *ribollita* (bean and/or cabbage soup which means "twice-cooked soup). *Chianti*, *chianti* and more *chianti*. Enough said!

UMBRIA (Assisi & the Hill Towns North of Rome)

Green hills, towns spared from industrialization, and wonderful dining combine to make Umbria an outstanding Italian destination (especially by car). Perugia is Umbria's largest city with a historic city center, but most tourists come here to visit the smaller towns like Gubbio in northern Umbria. Orvieto is located on a monumental square-shaped rock visible for miles. Don't miss this impressive and well-preserved town (or a taste of its famous wines). Assisi is home to a huge basilica built in memory of local hero St. Francis. It is ironic that such a huge basilica was built for such a humble man or that the streets are filled with shops selling St. Francis keychains. Still, Assisi, perched on a hill, is a memorable sight. Walled Spoleto (home of the well-known art festival) is dominated by a large castle and is surrounded by wooded countryside.

Tartufi (truffles) are a specialty here, especially the black truffle (*tartufo nero*). *Stringozzi* (homemade pasta) is used in many dishes, especially in Spoleto. *Strozzapreti* (dumplings with meat sauce) is a dish with the strange name of "priest stranglers" after a priest allegedly choked on it. *Palombacci* are small songbirds cooked whole on a spit. For dessert, try *stinchetti* (marzipan cakes). Of course, no one thinks of eating in Umbria without drinking one of the many fine wines of this region.

VENETO (Venice & its Environs)

Veneto is the region around Venice. Despite the tourists, the sometimes smelly canals and the often

inflated prices, Venice is unlike anywhere else in the world. Many cities claim to be pedestrian only, but Venice is truly car-free. Don't just take a day trip here. Once the day trippers leave, Venice becomes a quiet, romantic maze of streets with spectacular architecture. As many times as we have visited, we are always amazed at the splendid beauty of Venice with its buildings rising out of the sea. Don't miss the Piazza San Marco, the Bridge of Sighs, the Basilica di San Marco and the Doge's Palace. If time permits, visit the islands of Murano (famous for its ornate glass), Burano (famous for its lace), San Michele (Venice's island cemetery) and Torcello (for a taste of an almost deserted island).

Veneto includes the cities of Vicenza, Padua (where you can see the "uncorrupted" tongue of St. Anthony), Verona and Treviso. Many towns remain unspoiled and rarely visited by tourists, including Valpolicella (home of this popular Italian red wine), the hills of Colli Euganei (home of hot thermal springs), and Asolo. North of Treviso are the mountain resorts of Cortina d' Ampezzo and Belluno.

Cape sante (scallops), *baccalà* (dried cod), *fegato alla veneziana* (liver with onions), *seppie* (cuttlefish), and *granseola* (crab) are all specialties of Venice. *Polenta* (the famous cornmeal mush) is found throughout the region. *Carpaccio* is thinly sliced raw beef served in a sauce and was named by the owner of Harry's Bar in Venice after a famous Venetian painter. *Prosecco* is a slightly sparkling wine from Veneto and worth a try. While in Venice, don't miss having an evening drink or *caffè* in the Piazza San Marco.

26

Speaking Italian - Pronunciation Guide

If you are looking for a comprehensive guide to speaking Italian, this is not the the place. These are simply a few tips for speaking Italian followed by a very brief pronunciation guide. It is always good to learn a few polite terms so that you can excuse yourself when you've stepped on the foot of an elderly lady or spilled your drink down the back of the gentleman in front of you. It's also just common courtesy to greet the people you meet in your hotel, and in shops and restaurants, in their own language.

In Italian, you pronounce every letter. E and i are soft vowels when used with consonants. The final e is always pronounced.

The second to the last syllable is stressed. If there is an accent in the word, stress the accented syllable.

a like in father.
au like ow in cow.
b the same as in English.
c **ca, co** and **cu** like k in keep.
– **ce** and **ci**, like ch in cheap.
ch like k in kite.
d the same as in English.
e like in day.
ei like ay in lay.
f the same as in English.
g **ga, go** and **gu** like g in gate.
– **ge** and **gi** like j in jar.
gh like g in goat.
gl like gl in glow except before i, then like lli in million.
gn like ni in onion.
h silent. H after a consonant gives it a hard sound.
i like ee in jeep.
ie, io, iu, i is pronounced as y (ie. *pensione* ~ pen syo neh).
k/l/m/n the same as in English.
o usually like o in boat.

p/q the same as in English.
ue, ui, uo, the u is pronounced like a w (ie. *buono* ~ bwo no).
r with a slight trill.
s like s in sit except between two vowels, then like s in hose.
sc **sca, sco** or **scu** as sk in skirt.
– **sce** or **sci** as sh in sharp.
t the same as English.
u like oo in foot.
v the same as in English.
z the same as ds in fads.

Pronunciation

CA - KA
CE - CHAY
CI - CHEE
CHI - KEY
CHE - KAY

Confused?

This is a brief listing of some familiar English food and food-related words that you may need in a restaurant, followed by a list of phrases that may come in handy.

anchovy, acciuga (acciughe)
appetizer, antipasto (i)
apple, mela (e)
artichoke, carciofo (i)
ashtray, portacenere
asparagus, asparago (i)
bacon, pancetta
baked, al forno
banana, banana (e)
bean, fagiolo (i)
beef, manzo (di bue)
beefsteak, bistecca (di manzo)
beer, birra (e)
beverage, bevanda (e)
bill, conto (i)
bitter, amaro (a)
boiled, bollito/lesso
bottle, bottiglia
bowl, scodella
bread, pane
bread rolls, panino (i)
breakfast, prima colazione
broiled, graticola/griglia
broth, brodo
butter, burro
cabbage, cavolo (i)
cake, torta (e)
candle, candela
carrot, carota (e)
cereal, cereale (i)
chair, sedia

Words that end in A or O are singular

Words that end in E or I are plural

Carciofo ~ car CHEE off Foe

bottiglia ~ bow·tee·Lee-ah

Words and letters in parentheses indicate plurals.

Cereale ~ cheer·ee·ah·Lay

28

check, conto (i)
cheers, salute/cin cin
cheese, formaggio (formaggi)
cherry, ciliegia (e)
chicken soup, brodo di pollo/zuppa di pollo
chicken, pollo
chop, costoletta (e)
clam, vongola (e)
cocktail, cocktail
cod, baccalà/merluzzo
coffee, caffè (also black coffee)
**coffee w/hot water
  (to dilute),** caffè amercano
coffee w/milk, caffè latte
coffee (decaf), caffè hag/caffè decaffeinato
coffee w/cream, caffè con panna
cold, freddo (a)
corn, mais
cover charge, pane coperto
cucumber, cetriolo (i)
cup, coppa
  tazza coffee/tea cup
custard, crema
dessert, dolce (i)
dinner, cena
dish (plate), piatto
drink, bevanda (e)
dry (as in wine), secco
duck, anitra/anatra
egg, uovo (a)
espresso, caffè espresso
fish, pesce
fish soup, zuppa di pesce
fork, forchetta
french fries, patate fritte
fresh, fresco (a)
fried, fritto (a)/fritti (e)

caffè
italiano.

caffè
americano.

freddo ~
FRAY-doh

dolce ~
dole-chay

cena ~
Chain-ah

forchetta.

forchetta ~
FOR - KAY-TAH

fruit, frutta
game, cacciagione/selvaggina
garlic, aglio
gin, gin
glass, bicchiere
grapefruit, pompelmo
grape, uva
green bean, fagiolino (i)
grilled, griglia or alla griglia
half, mezzo (a)
ham (cooked), prosciutto cotto
ham (cured), prosciutto crudo
hamburger, hamburger
honey, miele
hors d'oeuvre, antipasto
hot, caldo (a)
iced, ghiacciato
ice coffee, caffè freddo
ice cream, gelato (i)
ice (on the rocks), ghiaccio or con ghiaccio
ice water, acqua fredda
iced tea, tè freddo
ketchup, ketchup/salsa di pomodoro
knife, coltello
lamb, abbacchio/agnello
large, grande
lemon, limone (i)
lettuce, lattuga
little (a little), un pó
liver, fegato (fegatini)
lobster, aragosta (e)
loin, lombata
lunch, pranzo
marinated, marinato (a)
match, fiammifero (i)
meat, carne
medium (cooked), a puntino or normale

Bicchiere.
BEE·KEE·AY·RAY

griglia
GREE-LEE·AH

ghiacciato ~
ghee-AH-chee-A·Tot

coltello.

melon, melone
menu, carta or menù
milk, latte
mineral water, acqua minerale
mineral water (sparkling), acqua minerale gasata
mineral water (w/out carbonation), acqua minerale non gasata
mixed, mista (o)
mushroom, fungo (i)
mussel, cozza (e)
mustard, senape
napkin, tovagliolo
noodles, taglierini/pasta
octopus, polipo/polpo
oil, olio
olive oil, olio d'oliva
omelette, frittata
on the rocks (w/ ice), con ghiaccio
onion, cipolla (e)
orange, arancia (arance)
orange juice, succo d'arancia
overdone, ben cotto
oyster, ostrica (ostriche)
pastries, dolci/paste
peach, pesca (pesche)
pear, pera (e)
pea, pisello (i)
pepper (black), pepe
pepper (bell), peperone (i)
perch, pesce persico
pineapple, ananas
plate (dish), piatto
please, per piacere
plum, susina (e)
poached, affogato
pork, maiale

funghi.

*Tovagliolo ~
Toe·vah·Lee·oh·Lo*

*cipolla ~
chee·polla*

*per piacere ~
Pare·pee·ah·chair·AY*

*maiale ~
my·AL·LAY*

potato, patata (e)
poultry, pollame
prawn, gamberetto (i)
rabbit, coniglio
rare, al sangue
raspberry, lampone (i)
receipt, ricevuta/scontrino
rice, riso
roast, arrosto
salad, insalata
salt, sale
sandwich, sandwich/panino (i)
sauce, salsa
saucer, piattino/sottocoppa
sautéed, saltato (i)/saltata (e)
scallops, cappe sante
scrambled, strapazzate
seafood, frutti di mare
seasoning, condimento (i)
shrimp, scampo (i),
    gamberetto (i)
small, piccolo (i)/piccola (e)
smoked, affumicata (o)
snail, lumaca (lumache)
sole, sogliola (e)
soup, zuppa (e)/minestra (e)
spaghetti, spaghetti
sparkling wine, spumante
specialty, specialità
spinach, spinaci
spoon, cucchiaio
squid, calamaro (i)
steak, bistecca
steamed, a vapore
stewed, in umido
strawberry, fragola (e)
sugar, zucchero

Coniglio.
Co-NEE-LEO

ricevuta ~
ree·chay·voo·tah

gamberetto.

Lumaca.

spaghetti ~
spa-get·tee

Cucchiaio ~
KOO KEE AYE OH

Zucchero ~
ZOO · KARE - OH

sugar substitute, dolcificante
supper, cena
sweet, dolce   *dolce* – DOL-CHAY
table, tavolo
tea, tè
tea w/lemon, tè al limone
tea w/milk, tè al latte
teaspoon, cucchiaino
thank you, grazie
tip, mancia
toasted, tostato
tomato, pomodoro (i)
trout, trota
tumbler (glass), bicchiere
tuna, tonno
turkey, tacchino
utensil, posata (e)/utensile (i)
veal, vitello
veal scallop, scaloppa di vitello
vegetable, legume (i). *Verdura (e)* green vegetables
vegetarian, vegetariana (o)
venison, carne di cervo
vinegar, aceto
waiter, cameriere
waitress, cameriera
water, acqua
well done, ben cotto
whipped cream, panna montata
wine, vino
wine (full-bodied), vino corposo
wine list, lista dei vini
wine (red), vino rosso
wine (rosé), vino rosé
wine (white), vino bianco

TAZZA
di
tè.

tacchino
TA-KEE-NO

Unless there's a written translation, it pretty much sounds like it looks, only more Italian sounding. Don't forget to pronounce that final 'E'!

Helpful Phrases

Prego can mean: thank you, you're welcome, this way (with a hand gesture), please, okay, and can I help you.

Ciao means hello *and* goodbye.

Italians answer the phone with *Pronto?*

please, per piacere/per favore
thank you, grazie
yes, sì
no, no
good morning, buon giorno
good afternoon/evening, buona sera
good night, buona notte
goodbye, arrivederci/ciao
do you speak English?, parla inglese?
I don't speak Italian, non parlo italiano
excuse me, mi scusi (or *scusi*)
I don't understand, non capisco
I'm hungry, Ho fame
I'm thirsty, Ho sete
I'd like..., Vorrei...
I'd like a table, please, Vorrei un tavolo, per piacere
I want to reserve a table, Vorrei prenotare un tavolo
for one person, per uno (una)
for two persons, per due

    tre (3)
    quattro (4)
    cinque (5)
    sei (6)
    sette (7)
    otto (8)
    nove (9),
    dieci (10)
this evening, stasera
tomorrow, domani

[handwritten annotations:]
non is pronounced almost like NONG.

Ho fame ~ OH Fah·may
Ho sete OH - SETTAY

OONO
DOO AY
TRAY
KWATRO
CHINK·WAY
SAY
SET·TAY
OH TOe
NO VAY
dee AY CHI

34

the day after tomorrow, dopodomani

near the window, vicino alla finestra

outside, fuori

inside, dentro

on the patio, sulla veranda

no smoking, zona per non fumatori

where is?, dov'è

the bathroom, il bagno/la toilette

the bill please, il conto, per piacere

a mistake, errore

is service included?, é incluso il servizio?

do you accept credit cards?, Posso pagare con una carta di credito?

how much does this cost?, quanto costa?

what is this?, cos' è questo?

this is not what I ordered, non ho ordinato questo

this is, questo è...

too, troppo

a little, un po'

cold, freddo (a)

hot, caldo (a)

spicy, piccante

not fresh, non è fresco

undercooked, troppo crudo

overcooked, troppo cotto/stracotto

very good, molto buono

delicious, delizioso (a)

diet, dieta

closed, chiuso (a)

Monday, lunedì

Tuesday, martedì

Wednesday, mercoledì

Thursday, giovedì

Friday, venerdì

Saturday, sabato

Sunday, domenica

Handwritten notes:
VICINO ~ VEE CHEE NO
fuori ~ FOO OH REE
Right - good Luck on that one.
freddo ~ FRAY-doh
chiuso ~ KEE-YOU-ZO

abbacchio, lamb

abbacchio alla cacciatora, pieces of lamb braised w/rosemary, garlic, wine & peppers

abbacchio alla romana, pieces of lamb cooked until brown, then roasted in a rosemary, garlic, vinegar & anchovy sauce

abbacchio brodettato, pieces of lamb cooked in a broth of lemon, parsley & beaten eggs

abboccato, a medium-sweet wine

abbrustolito, toasted

abruzzese, red pepper sauce

acciuga (acciughe), anchovy

acciuga ~
AH·CHEE·oo·ga

acciughe al limone, anchovies w/lemon-based sauce

acerbo, sour

aceto, vinegar

aceto balsamico, balsamic vinegar. Aged vinegar used in many dishes, especially salads

acetosella, sorrel

acido, sour

acini di pepe, pasta for soup in the shape of peppercorns

acqua, water

acqua brillante, tonic water

acquacotta, bread & vegetable soup

acquadella, small whitebait fish

"Acqua cotta"
means
cooked water

acqua di rubinetto, tap water

acqua di seltz, seltzer water/soda water

acqua fredda, ice water

acqua gasata, carbonated water

acqua ghiacciata, ice water

acqua minerale, mineral water

acqua minerale frizzante, extremely carbonated water

acqua minerale naturale, mineral water w/out carbonation

acqua naturale, tap water

acqua non gasata, water w/out carbonation

acqua non potabile, do not drink the water!

acqua pazza, sauce of tomato, garlic, oil, parsley & chili pepper

acqua semplice, tap water

acqua tonica, tonic water

Acquavite, brandy/distilled spirit flavored w/caraway

affettato, sliced

affettato (i), cold cut
affogato, poached. This can also refer
   to ice cream soaked in
   coffee or liqueur
affumicato, smoked
agliata/all'aglio, garlic sauce
aglio, garlic
aglio e olio, w/garlic & olive oil
agnello, lamb
agnello alla turca, lamb stew w/raisins
agnello con salsa di uovo, lamb w/egg
   sauce. A specialty in Le Marche
agnolotti, filled pasta (square shaped)
agone, freshwater fish found in the lake country
   (the size of sardines)
agresto, juice of unripened grapes
agro, lemon juice & olive oil dressing
agrodolce, sweet & sour sauce
ai/al/all'/alla, in the style of/with
ajula, sea bream
ala, wing
alaccia, large sardine
alalunga, albacore (a type of tuna)
Albana, dry to semi-sweet wine from Emilia-Romagna
albicocca (albicocche), apricot
albume, egg white
alcolica, alcoholic. *Una bevanda alcolica* is an alcoholic beverage
alcool, alcol
Aleatico, dessert wine (made from muscat grapes)
alette, wing
alfabetini, alphabet noodles for soup
al forno, baked
alfredo, w/butter & cream sauce
al fresco, outside (in the fresh air)
alice (i), anchovy
allodola (e), lark
alloro, bay leaf
amabile, slightly sweet wine
amarena (e), sour cherry
amaretti, macaroons
amaretto, sweet almond-flavored liqueur
amaro, bitter/bitter cordial (bitters)
amatriciana, bacon, tomato & spices sauce

Aglio.

*Agresto is
sometimes
used in
place of
vinegar*

ALLORO.

amburghese/amburgo, hamburger/ground meat

amburghese alla tirolese, hamburger served w/onion rings

Americano, Campari, vermouth & lemon peel

ammiru, prawns in Sicily

analcolico (i), non-alcoholic

ananas, pineapple

anatra, duck

anatroccolo, duckling

anelli/anellini, small circular pasta for soup (ring pasta)

aneto, dill

anguidda, another name for eel in Sicily

anguilla (e), eel

anguilla alla veneziana, eel braised w/tuna & lemon sauce

anguria, watermelon

anice, anise

animelle, sweetbreads

animelle alla salvia, sweetbreads w/sage

anisetta, anise-flavored liquor

anitra, duck

anitra germano, mallard duck

anitra selvatica, wild duck

annegati, slices of meat in wine

antipasto (i), appetizer

antipasto alla marinara/antipasto di mare/antipasto di pesce, assorted seafood

antipasto misto, assorted appetizers

aperitivo, aperitif

arachide (i), peanut

aragosta (e), lobster (crayfish)

arancia (e), orange. *All' arancia* means w/orange juice

aranciata, orangeade/orange soda

arancini, deep-fried rice balls

arancio di riso, cooked ball of rice stuffed w/meat & breaded & fried. This gets its name from the orange size of the ball

argentina, argentine fish

arigusta, crayfish

aringa, herring

aringa affumicata, smoked herring

arista, roast, seasoned pork loin

arista alla fiorentina, roasted pork rubbed w/garlic paste, cloves, salt, rosemary, pepper

In Perugia Anguilla can also refer to an eel shaped pastry created originally by nuns.

arista di maiale/arista di suino, pork loin

arrabbiata, all', w/a spicy tomato & herb sauce

arrostetti, small roast

arrosti misti freddi, a selection of cold roasted meats

arrostini, veal chops

arrostino, small roast

arrostino annegato, small veal roast
served with mushrooms

arrostite, grilled/roasted

arrosto/arrostito, roast/roasted

arrosto alla genovese, a roast w/onions, mushrooms
& tomatoes

arrosto alla montanara, pot roast

arrosto con pastine, roast w/dough crust

arrosto di manzo, roast beef

arrosto in porchetta, roast suckling pig stuffed w/garlic,
bacon & herbs

arrosto misto, mixed roast meats

arrosto morto, pot roast

arsella (e), mussel

asciutta (o), dry. Also refers to pasta w/sauce
(as opposed to pasta for soup)

asiago, sharp cheese (round-shaped cheese)

asiago dolce, mild *asiago*

asparago (i), asparagus

asparago alla bismark, asparagus w/melted butter & fried egg

asparago alla milanese/asparago all'uovo, asapagus topped
w/melted butter, *parmesan* cheese & fried egg

assortito (i), assorted

astice (i), prawn/lobster

Asti Spumante, sparkling white wine

attorta, fruit & almond-filled pastry

Aurum, orange liqueur

avvoltino, standing roast or rolled roast

babà, spongecake covered w/rum

babaluci, snails in tomato & onion sauce

bacca (e), berry

baccalà, salt cod

ASTI.

baccalà alla fiorentina, salt cod floured & fried in oil
& tomato sauce

baccalà alla lucana, salt cod cooked w/peppers

baccalà alla vicentina, salt cod w/onion, parsley, garlic,
anchovies & cinnamon

bacio, chocolate hazelnut (means "kiss")
bagna cauda/bagna caoda, hot vegetable dip w/anchovies
bagnet, sauce (in Piedmont)
balsamella, bechamel/white sauce
banana (e), banana *Good Guess!*
bar, serves espresso, cappuccino, rolls, small sandwiches,
    alcoholic beverages and soft drinks
barbabietola (e), beet
Barbaresco, soft red wine from Piedmont
    (lighter & drier than *Barolo*)
Barbera, dry red wine
barbe rosse, beets
Bardolino, pale, light red wine
Barolo, rich red wine from Piedmont

Andy hates beets even in Italy.

basilico, basil
bastoncini, bread sticks (means "little sticks")
battuta scanello, pounded round steak
battutina al prosciutto, hamburger mixed w/cured ham
battuto, finely chopped herbs,
    onions, celery & carrots
battuto di manzo, ground beef
bavette (i), thin, flat pasta
beccaccia, woodcock
beccaccino, snipe (game)
beccafico, warbler/song bird
belga, Belgian endive
bellini, sparkling wine & peach juice
bel paese, smooth, mild & soft cheese
ben cotta, well done
bensone, lemon cake

"Bel Paese" means beautiful country

besciamella, white cream sauce
bevanda (e), drink/beverage
bevanda compresa, cost of drinks included
bianchetti, small anchovy (or sardine)
bianchi, white
bianco, white wine
Bianco di Martina, a fortified wine found in Apulia
bianco, in, w/butter (w/out a sauce)
bibita (e), drink/beverage
bibite analcoliche, soft drinks
bicchiere, glass
biete, Swiss chard
bietole, beet/Swiss chard

Bicchiere.
BEE·KEE·AY·RAY

bietole alla padella, Swiss chard cooked w/butter &/or oil

bietoline, beet greens

bietolini, Swiss chard

bignè/bignole (con crema), cream puff

bigoli, larger form of spaghetti

biova/biovetta, round bread loaf

birra, beer

birra alla spina, tap beer

birra analcolica, no-alcohol beer

birra bionda, light beer

birra chiara, light beer (lager)

birra di barile, draft beer

birra importata, imported beer

birra in bottiglia, bottled beer

BiRRA

birra in lattina, beer in a can

birra scura, dark beer

biscotto (i), cookie/biscuit/cracker/spongecake

biscotti di prato, cookies w/pieces of almond

biscuit tortoni, dessert of beaten egg whites & macaroon
crumbs topped w/whipped cream & toasted almonds

bismark, alla, usually means served w/a fried egg

bistecca, steak

bistecca alla bismark, fried steak w/an egg on top

bistecca alla fiorentina, T-bone steak

bistecca alla pizzaiola, steak w/tomato & garlic sauce

bistecca di manzo, beef steak

bistecca di vitello, veal scallop

bistecca Fiorentina, T-bone steak

bistecca impanata, cutlet/chop

bistecche, steaks

bistecchine, thin steaks

bitto, firm, smoked cheese

bobe, sea bream

boccolotti, short tubular pasta

bocconcini, diced veal w/tomato
& white wine sauce/*mozzarella* balls

Bistecca Impanata is often breaded and fried in butter

boldro, monkfish in Tuscany

boletus, porcini mushrooms

"bocconcini" means mouthful

bollito (i), boiled. Can also mean meat or fish stew

bollito di gallina, boiled chicken

bollito di manzo, boiled beef

bollito misto, mixed boiled meats

bolognese, alla, usually means a tomato & meat sauce

bomba di riso, rice dish w/ground meat & herb fillings
bombolone (i), doughnut
bonèt, chocolate cream dessert. A specialty in Piedmont
borlotti, type of bean
boscaiola, means "woodsman style" & can refer to many
    things, including w/wild mushrooms
bosega, mullet
botolo, mullet
bottarga, fish eggs (tuna roe that has been salted & pressed)
bottiglia, bottle
bove, beef
bovoletti/bovoloni, small snails in Venice
brace, alla, on charcoal
braciola (e), rib steak/chop/cutlet
braciola di maiale, pork chop
bracioletta, small slice of meat
bracioletta a scottadito, lamb chops (charcoal grilled)
bracioline/braciolone, meat roll
braciolone alla napoletana, breaded steak, rolled & stewed
brandy, brandy
branzino, bass
branzinotti, small sea bass
brasato, braised/braised meat w/wine
bresaola, thinly sliced cured raw beef
briciole di pane, breadcrumbs
brioche, buns/rolls/small loaf (used for breakfast)
broccoletti, broccoli
broccoletti di rape, turnip greens
broccoletti strascinati, broccoli sautéed w/garlic & bacon
broccolo (i), broccoli
brodetto, rich fish soup
brodo, broth/soup/bouillon.
    In brodo means cooked in broth
brodo di manzo, consomme/beef broth
brodo di pollo, chicken soup
brogue, sea bream
brovada, marinated turnips w/pork sausage
Brunello, full-bodied red wine from Montalcino
bruschetta, grilled bread w/garlic & olive oil (frequently
    topped w/tomatoes &/or onions)
brut, very dry wine
brutti, small almond cakes
bucaniera, tomato & garlic seafood sauce

Handwritten annotations: bottiglia~ / Bow-Tee-Lee AH / Broccolo. / Bucaniera... Buccaneer, get it?

bucatini, hollow spaghetti noodles
bucatoni, same as *bucatini*, but larger
budino, custard/pudding
budino alla toscana, cream cheese w/raisins, almonds,
   sugar & egg yolks
bue, beef
burrata, a very buttery cheese found in Apulia
burrida, fish stew or casserole. In Sardinia this refers to a
   poached & marinated fish dish
burrini, a type of hard, aged cheese
burro, butter
burro maggiordomo, butter w/lemon
   juice & parsley
busecca, tripe & vegetable soup
buttiri, a type of hard, aged cheese
cacao, cocoa
cacasor cioccolata, cocoa
cacciagione, game
cacciatora, alla/cacciatore, w/mushrooms,
   wine, tomatoes & herbs
cacciucco, spicy fish soup
cachi, persimmons
caciatella, a crème caramel dessert
cacio, *pecorino* cheese
caciocavallo, a hard, aged cheese
   made of whole milk
cacio e pepe, sauce made of
   black pepper & *pecorino* cheese
cacio e uova, w/cheese & egg
caciotta, mild cheese
caciucco, fish soup
caffè, coffee
caffè al vetro, coffee served in a glass
caffè americano, American-style coffee (Italian coffee diluted
   w/hot water)
caffè con panna, coffee w/cream
caffè corretto, *espresso* w/a shot of liquor (usually brandy)
caffè doppio, coffee (a double serving)
caffè espresso, *espresso*
caffè freddo, iced coffee
caffè hag, decaffeinated coffee
caffè latte, coffee w/steamed milk
caffè lungo, coffee w/water (weaker coffee)

alla cacciatora means in the style of the hunter

Traditionally there must be as many types of fish in the soup as c's in cacciucco.

caffè macchiato, coffee w/a small amount of warm milk
caffè nero, black coffee
caffè ristretto, small, thick & strong
   coffee (stronger than an *espresso*)
calamaretto (i), small squid
calamari, squid
calamari fritti, fried squid
calamito, grey mullet
caldo (a)/caldi (e), warm or hot
caldaro, fish & potato soup
calzone (i), folded & stuffed pizza
cameriera, waitress
cameriere, waiter
camicia, in, poached
camomilla, camomile tea
camoscio, small deer (chamois)
campagnola, alla, w/vegetables & herbs
Campari, red aperitif w/a bitter, quinine taste
campo, del, wild. *Cicoria del campo* is wild chicory
candita (o), candied
canederli, dumplings made w/ham, sausage & breadcrumbs
canestrelli, sweet pastry/small sea snail or scallop
cannella, cinnamon
cannellini, small white beans found in Tuscany
cannelloni, large tube pasta stuffed w/fillings
cannelloni al forno, stuffed & browned in oven
cannelloni alla Barbaroux, stuffed w/ham, veal & cheese
cannelloni alla laziale, stuffed w/meat & onions
cannelloni alla napoletana, stuffed w/ham & cheese
   w/tomato & herb sauce
cannelloni alla piemontese, stuffed w/veal, ham & cheese
cannocchie, see *canoce*
cannoli alla siciliana, *ricotta* cheese-filled pastry
   w/sugar glaze
cannolicchio, razor-shell clam
cannolo (i), custard-filled pastry w/candied fruit or sweet
   white cheese (*ricotta*). This
   also refers to a short pasta tube
canoce, Venetian word for
   cannocchie which is neither a
   shrimp nor a lobster but something in between
cantarello, chanterelle mushroom

caffè.

cantarello.

cantucci, almond biscuits

capelli d'angelo, thin noodle soup ("angel hair")

capellini, long, thin, fine spaghetti

capelunghe, razor clams

cape sante, scallops in Venice

capitone, large eel

capocollo, smoked pork salami

caponata, cold dish of eggplant & vegetables.
   Eggplant, celery & onions are fried separately &
   cooked in a sweet & sour sauce of raisins, tomatoes,
   pine nuts, sugar & vinegar

caponata di melanzane, eggplant & pepper stew

cappelle di funghi, mushroom caps

cappelletti, rings of pasta filled w/ground meat.
   Some think they look like little caps

cappello da prete, a triangular
   sausage ("priest's hat")

cappero (i), caper

cappesante, scallops (means
   "sacred shells")

capponcello ruspante al forno,
   roast farm-raised capon

cappone, capon

cappon magro, vegetables & fish stacked high on a plate

cappuccino, coffee w/steamed milk

capra, goat

caprese, *mozzarella* & tomatoes. ***Pasta caprese*** is pasta
   w/tomatoes, *mozzarella* & basil. *Caprese* means
   from the island of Capri

capretto, baby goat

capretto al forno, roasted kid stuffed w/herbs

capretto alla pasqualina, roasted baby goat (an Easter dish)

capricciosa (o), chef's special (means "caprice" or "whim")

caprino, mild goat's-milk cheese

caprino fresco, a fresh goat's-milk cheese

caprino romano, hard goat's-milk cheese

capriolo, small deer (roebuck)

caraffa, carafe

caramellate, caramelized

caramella (e), candy (not chocolate)

caramello, caramel

carbonade, beef cooked in wine & onions

carbonara, pasta w/bacon (or ham), cheese, olive oil & eggs

[handwritten margin note: "Cappello da prete" means priest's hat.]

45

carbonata, grilled pork chop. Sometimes this
refers to beef stew in red wine

carciofi alla giudea, deep-fried artichokes
(prepared in the shape of a rose).
This term means "Jewish-style artichokes"

carciofi alla romana, artichokes stuffed w/garlic, parsley &
mint & cooked in olive oil & white wine

carciofi in pinzimonio, raw artichokes in an oil dressing

carciofini in umido, artichole hearts sautéed in garlic & tomatoes

carciofini sott'olio, artichokes in olive oil

carciofino (i), small artichoke

carciofo (i), artichoke. The bottoms of artichokes are the *fondi
di carciofi*

cardo (i), cardoon, a vegetable that looks like celery
but tastes like artichokes

carciofo.

carne, meat

carne a carrargiu, spit-roasted meat

carne cruda all`albese, slices of raw steak

carne di cervo, venison

carne macinata, ground meat

carne per arrosto in pentola, pot roast

carne tritata, ground meat

carone, large white beans

carota (e), carrot

carpa/carpione, carp

carpaccio, thinly sliced raw beef w/sauce. Named by the owner
of Harry's Bar in Venice after a famous Venetian painter

carpaccio di branzino, slices of raw sea bass w/a sauce

carpione, in, served cold w/vinegar sauce

carrargiu, spit-roasted

carré, sliced bread ("square")   *"Carré" means
square.*

carrè di..., roast loin of...

carrello, al, served from the food cart

carrettiera, tuna, garlic & pork sauce

carruba, carob

carta, menu

carta da musica, flat, crispy bread of Sardinia. See *pane carasau*

carteddate/cartellate, fried pastry dipped in honey

cartoccio, al, roasted (often in a paper bag, foil or other
covering). The covering is opened at the table

carvi (grani di), caraway (seeds)

casa, house. *Della casa* means "house specialty"

casalinga (o), homemade

cascà, the Sardinian version of couscous

casoncelli, pasta stuffed w/ground meat

cassata, ice cream (or sweet *ricotta* cheese) w/candied fruit

cassata alla siciliana, *ricotta* cheese-filled layered cake
   w/sugar glaze

cassata gelata, various flavors of ice cream w/candied fruit

casserola/casseruola, casserole

cassoela/cassoeula, pork casserole

castagna (e), chestnut

castagnaccio, chestnut cake

castagnole, chestnut fritters

castellana, stuffed veal cutlet

Castelli Romani, white table wine
   from the area southeast of Rome

Cavoletti:

castrato, mutton

catalogna, a type of salad green (like spinach, often cooked)

cauladda, Sardinian soup of cabbage, beans, sausage & meats

cavalla, mackerel. Also refers to a female horse

cavatappi, tubular pasta in the shape of a corkscrew

cavatelli/cavatieddi, homemade pasta

caviale, caviar

caviale del sud, "caviar of the south." Calabrian dish of dried
   small fish preserved in oil & powdered w/*peperoncino*

cavoletti, Brussels sprouts

cavolfiore, cauliflower

cavolini di Bruxelles/cavoli di Brusselle, Brussels sprouts

cavolo (i), cabbage

cavolo broccoluto, broccoli

cavolo riccio, kale

cavolo rosso, red cabbage

cavolo verde, green cabbage

cazzoeula, pork casserole

cecatelli, homemade pasta

cece (i), chickpea/garbanzo

ceche, baby eels

EELS BREED in fresh water & mature in the sea.

ceci alla Pisana, chickpea stew

cedrata/cedro, a large fruit that resembles a lemon.
   The peel is used for flavoring

cee alla Pisana, baby-eel dish from Pisa

cefalo, grey mullet

cena, dinner

*cena –
chain-ah*

cenci, fried pastry

Centerbe, green herb liqueur

cèpes, porcini mushroom

Cerasella, cherry liqueur

cereale, cereal

cerfoglio, chervil

cernia, grouper

Certosino, green or yellow herb liqueur.
  This is also the name for a soft & mild cheese

cervella, brains

cervo, venison

cestino di frutta, a basket of fruit

cetriolino (i), pickle

cetriolo (i), cucumber

cevapcici, grilled meatballs found near Italian/Slovenian border

champagne, champagne

charlotte, spongecake & whipped-cream dessert

Chianti, well-known medium-bodied red wine from Tuscany.
  Chianti Classico comes from the center of the Chianti
  region, is aged for at least one year & is more complex.
  Riserva denotes a *Chianti* aged for at least two years

chiare, egg whites

Chiaretto, young & popular rosé wine

chifferi, "c"-shaped tubular pasta

chiocciola (e), snail/sea shell-shaped pasta

chiocciolina, little snail

chiocciolini, spiral-shaped buns

chiodi di garofani, cloves

chiodino (i) a type of mushroom

chiodo di garofano, clove

ciabatta, large, coarse bread loaf

ciauscolo, soft, fatty pork sausage

cialda (e), waffle/wafer

cialledda, vegetable soup w/bread, olives, tomato, hard-boiled
  eggs & olive oil. A specialty in Basilicata

cialsons/chialzons, sweet & sour pasta

ciambella/chiambella/ciambelline, donut (not fried like North
  American donuts)

cibo, food

cibreo, chicken-liver dish

cicale di mare, type of shrimp (this crustacean is found off the
  coast of Italy. The name means "grasshopper")

ciccheti/cicheti, snacks served in Venice (similar to Spanish *tapas*)

cicina, mixture of small fried fish

cicoria, chicory/endive

ciliegia (e), cherry

cima, stuffed veal served cold

cima alla genovese, veal stuffed w/mushrooms & sausage

cimalino, *cima* served w/beans. **Cimalino di manzo** is stuffed breast of beef

cime di rape, turnip greens

cinese, Chinese

cinghiale, boar

Cinque Terre, a dry, light white wine from the spectacularly beautiful five towns on the western coast of Italy

cioccolata, chocolate

cioccolata calda, hot chocolate

cioccolato, chocolate (hot chocolate)

ciociara, a seasoned meat sauce

cioppino, fish stew (this word is usually used only in the United States)

cipolla (e), onion

cipollina (e), chive

cipolline novelle, green onions

cipollotti, spring onions

ciriola, small eel

ciuppin, thick fish (& vegetable) soup

civraxin, Sardinian large bread loaf

cocco/noce di cocco, coconut

cocktail di vongole, clam cocktail (clams, olive oil & lemon)

cocktail martini, martini

cocomero, watermelon

cocozelle, zucchini

coda, tail

coda alla vaccinara, oxtail stew in a tomato & garlic sauce

Cocomero.

coda di bue, oxtail

coda di rospo, monkfish

cognac, cognac

colazione (prima), breakfast

collo, neck

colomba, dove-shaped cake. **Colombo** means pigeon

colombacchi, wild pigeon

coltello, knife

composta, stewed fruit (compote)

composta cotta, mixed cold, cooked vegetables

con, with

conchiglie, shell-shaped pasta. *Conchigliette* is a small version used in soup

condimento (i), condiment

confetti, sugared almonds (used in weddings & special occasions)

confettura, jam

con ghiaccio, on the rocks

coniglio, rabbit

coniglio all'agro, rabbit stewed in red wine

coniglio all'Anconetana, a stuffed-rabbit dish

cono, cone (as in ice cream cone)

con seltz, w/soda

conserva, preserves/jam/jelly

conserva di frutta, preserves/jam/jelly

consommè, consomme (clear soup)

consommè madrilena, clear tomato soup

consommè reale, chicken consomme

Coniglio.
Co-NEE-LEO

contadina, alla, usually means served in a tomato & mushroom sauce (means "peasant woman")

conto, check/bill

contorno (i), side dish/garnish. This often refers to a vegetable side dish

contrafiletto/controfiletto, sirloin

copata, honey & nut wafer

coperto, cover charge

coppa, cup/goblet/small bowl. *Coppa* can also refer to smoked ham or smoked bacon

coppa di frutta, fruit cup/fruit cocktail

coppa di gamberetti, shrimp cocktail

coppa gelato, cup of ice cream/sundae

coratella di abbacchio, lamb heart, lung & liver dish

corda, lamb-tripe dish

cordulla, Sardinian dish made w/intestines

coregone, a type of salmon

coriandolo, coriander

cornetti, string beans

cornetto, croissant

corona, large white bean

'Cornetto' means trumpet.

corposo, full-bodied wine

corretto, coffee or *espresso*
w/a shot of alcohol

Cortese, dry white wine

Corvo, dry, light white wine from Sicily

cosce di rana, frogs' legs

coscetta, leg/drumstick

coscia, leg

cosciette di rane, frogs' legs

cosciotto, leg

cosciotto di agnello, leg of lamb

cosciotto di porcello, leg of young lamb

costa, rib/scallop

costa di manzo, rib roast/T-bone steak

costa di sedano, celery stalk

costarelle di abbacchio a scottadito, grilled lamb cutlet

costarelli, spareribs/pork chops

costata, chop/beef steak. *Costata di vitello* is a veal chop.
Costata di manzo is rib steak

costata alla fiorentina, grilled beef steak

costata alla pizzaiola, braised beef steak in a tomato sauce &
mozzarella cheese

costate, rib steaks

costate d'agnello, rack of lamb

costatella, rib steak

costellata/costelleta/
costelletine, rib steak

costicini, pork spareribs

costine, pork spareribs

costola arrostita, rib roast

costolatura, beef loin

costole di manzo, prime rib

We have found that European cuts of meat often look nothing like cuts of the same name in the States.

costoletta (e), cutlet/chop (often coated in eggs & breadcrumbs
& fried in butter)

costoletta alla bolognese, breaded veal cutlet w/tomato sauce,
cheese & ham

costoletta alla milanese, breaded & fried veal cutlet

costoletta alla parmigiana, cutlet breaded & baked w/
parmesan cheese

costoletta alla siciliana, thin slices of veal or beef topped
w/chopped garlic & *parmesan* cheese, breaded & deep-fried

costoletta alla valdostana, cutlet w/ham & cheese stuffing

51

costoletta alla viennese, wiener schnitzel
costoletta di vitello impanata, breaded veal cutlet
costolette di tonno, tuna steaks
costolette di vitello, veal chops
costolettine, lamb or pork chop
cotechino/coteghino, spicy pork sausage
cotognata, quince marmalade
cotogne, quince
cotoletta (e), cutlet, usually a veal cutlet
cotoletta alla bolognese, breaded veal cutlet topped w/ham,
    cheese & tomato sauce
cotto, cooked
cotto antico, bay leaf-flavored salami
cotto a puntino, medium done
courgette, zucchini
cozza (e), mussel
cozze alla marinara, mussels in white wine, garlic & parsley
cozze Posillipo, mussels in a spicy tomato sauce
crauti, sauerkraut
crema, cream/custard
crema caramella, custard w/caramelized-sugar topping
crema da montare, whipping cream
crema di, cream of
crema di funghi, cream of mushroom soup
crema di piselli, cream of pea soup
crema di pollo, cream of chicken soup
crema di verdura, puree of vegetables
crema fritta, fried-custard dessert
crema inglese, custard w/stewed fruit or cake
crème caramel, caramel custard
cremini, a type of mushroom
cremino, ice cream bar/a soft cheese
cren, horseradish
crescenza, a soft, buttery cheese (w/relatively low fat content)
crescionda, Umbrian dessert made from amaretto cookies,
    eggs, milk & unsweetened cocoa
crescione/crescione di fonte, watercress
crespelle, crêpes
crespelle alla fiorentina, spinach crêpes
crespolino, meat-filled pancake
croccheta (e), croquette
crocchette di patate, potato croquettes

Courgette is actually a french word found on menus near the french border.

crocchette di riso, deep-fried rice balls w/cheese in the center

crosta, crust (as in a pie crust)

crostaceo (i), shellfish

crostata, open-faced pie

crostata di frutta, fruit pie

crostini/crostoni, bread, fried or toasted in oil & topped w/many ingredients/croutons

crostini alla napoletana, toast w/cheese & anchovies

crostini alla provatura, toasted diced bread w/*provatura* cheese

crostini di mare, shellfish on fried bread

crostini di milza, toast w/veal paté

crostini Fiorentina, toast w/liver paté

crostini in brodo, croutons in broth

crostone di polenta, roasted meat (usually game) served on a round base of *polenta*

crudo, raw

crusca, bran. This also refers to a bread found in Ticino w/thick crust & dusted w/flour

cubbaita, nougat w/almonds, honey & sesame seeds

cucchiaio, spoon

cuccia, layered dish of slow-roasted meats, tomato sauce & grains. A specialty in Calabria

cucina, cuisine

"cucina" means kitchen and cooking

culaccio, rump meat

culatello, ham cured in white wine

cumino, cumin

cunillu, Sardinian word for rabbit

cuoco, chef

cuore (i), heart

cuore di sedano, celery heart

cuori di carciofi, artichoke hearts

curry, curry

cuscusu di Trapani, couscous

Cynar, after-dinner drink made of artichokes

daino, deer

da portar via, to go

datteri di mare, mussels

dattero (i), date

decaffeinato, decaffeinated

"Decaffeinato" is becoming more common but be prepared for a condescending smile.

del giorno, of the day

della casa, of the house

53

dente, al, pasta cooked until it is still slightly firm
(means "to the tooth")

dentice, a Mediterranean fish (dentex) similar to sea bream

denti d'elefante, tubular pasta (like *macaroni*)
(means "elephant's tooth")

di, of

diavola/diavolicchio, usually means served w/pepper or chili
peppers. Can also mean a dish cooked over a flame since
the terms mean "devil"

digestivo, after-dinner drink

diavolo - devil

disossata, boned rib steak

di stagione, in season

ditali, small tubular pasta for soup,
often called thimbles. *Ditalini* is the
smaller version of this pasta

diverso, varied

dolce (i), dessert/sweet/pastry. *Dolce* can also mean sweet wine

Dolcetto, fruity, dry red wine from Piedmont

dolci di Taglierini, sweetened noodle (taglierini) cake

dolcificante, artificial sweetener

dorato (a), browned/golden brown

Doria, alla, w/cucumbers

e means and.

dragoncello, tarragon

é with an accent

e, and

means is.

eliche, spiral pasta.
Often refered to as propellers

elicoidali, tubular pasta w/straight edges

emmenthal, Swiss cheese

empanata, breaded

entrecìte/entrecote di bue, boneless rib steak

erbazzone, vegetable pie

erbe, herbs

erbette, cooked greens

espresso, *espresso* (strong, small coffee)

espresso doppio, a double serving of *espresso*

espresso macchiato, *espresso* w/a small amount of foamy milk
on top. Compare this to *latte macchiato*

Est Est Est, a dry, semi-sweet white wine

Etna, red & white Sicilian wines

etto, fish dishes are frequently served by the *etto*
(or 100 grams)

fagianella, bustard (bird)

fagiano, pheasant

fagioli al fiasco, slow-cooked Tuscan bean dish served w/garlic, herbs & olive oil

fagioli alla maruzzara, beans in an oregano & tomato sauce

fagioli all'Uccelloto, white beans in a tomato sauce

fagioli bianchi, white beans

fagioli bianco di Spagna, lima beans

fagioli cannellini, small white beans

fagioli con le cotiche, beans in a tomato sauce w/slices of pork

fagioli cotti al forno, baked beans

fagioli freschi, fresh beans

fagioli lessati al forno, boiled baked beans

fagioli lessi, shelled, boiled beans

fagiolino (i) green bean/French bean

fagioli rampicanti, runner beans

fagioli rossi, red kidney beans

fagioli sgranati, fresh shelled beans

fagioli toscani, cooked white-bean dish

fagioli verdi, green beans

fagiolo (i), bean

fagottini, food wrapped around a filling

Falerno, dry white & red wines

fame, hungry

faraona, guinea fowl

farcito (a), stuffed

farfalle/farfallette, bow-tie or butterfly-shaped pasta

farfalline (i), bow-tie or butterfly-shaped pasta

farina, flour

farinata, baked pancake made from olive oil, chickpea flour, salt & pepper (eaten as a snack)

farricello, barley

farro, red bean & barley porridge

farsumagru, veal or beef roll stuffed w/ham, bacon, cheese, onions & parsley. A Sardinian specialty

fasolini, scallops

fatto in casa, homemade

fava (e), broad bean. Sometimes called *fave grande* or *fave España*

favarella, bean soup

favata, bean, sausage & bacon casserole

fave al Guanciale, broad beans cooked w/bacon & onions

fagioli.

farfalle.

farricello.

fave e cicoria, pureéd fava beans, sauteéd chicory &
olive oil. A specialty in Apulia

fegà, liver in Venice

fegatelli di maiale, pork liver

fegato (fegatini), liver.
Fegatini di maiale are pork livers;
fegatini di pollo are chicken livers

fegato alla veneziana, liver & onions

fegato di vitello, calf's liver

Fernet, a bitter digestive liqueur

ferri, ai, sliced & grilled (means "on iron")

fesa, leg of veal

fesa in gelatina, roast veal w/aspic jelly

fetta di/fette di, slice of...

fettina, small slice

fettuccine (i), long, flat, thin ribbon noodle

fettuccine Alfredo, thin ribbon noodles w/cream, butter & nutmeg

fettuccine alla Panna, thin ribbon noodles w/cream, butter &
nutmeg

fettuccine in brodo, noodle soup

fettuna, toasted or grilled over an
open fire w/garlic & olive oil

fettura di melacotogne, quince jam

fiamma, alla, flamed

fiammifero (i), match

fianco, flank

fiasco, straw-covered flask

fichi d'India/fichi indiani, prickly pears

fichi in sciroppo, figs in syrup

fichi mandorlati, figs stuffed w/almonds

fico (fichi), fig

fidelanza, spaghetti in tomato
sauce in Liguria

filetti (di pomodoro), a sauce of sliced tomatoes

filetto (i), fillet or tenderloin

filu e ferru, Sardinian *grappa*

finferlo, an orange-colored mushroom

finocchiata, pork cured w/fennel & pepper

finocchio, fennel (some think fennel has a licorice flavor)

finocchiona, fennel-flavored salami

fiocchetto, cold cut made from the leg of pork

fiocchi, flakes

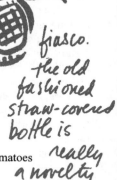

liver in venice, liver in milwaukee... No grazie

fiasco. the old fashioned straw-covered bottle is really a novelty now.

fiocchi di granoturco, cornflakes
fiocco, ham shoulder
fior di latte, *mozzarella* made from cow's milk
fiore, flower
fiorentina, alla, w/oil, tomatoes & herbs
  (sometimes w/peas or spinach)
fiori con ripieno, stuffed zucchini flowers
fiori di zucca, zucchini flowers served either filled w/cheese,
  battered & fried or as a pizza topping
fiori di zucca fritti, fried zucchini flowers
flambé, flamed
focaccia, flat bread topped w/olive oil & sometimes cheese
  &/or onions. Can also mean cake
focaccia barese, stuffed pizza. A specialty of Apulia
focaccia di vitello, veal patty
foglia (e), leaf
foglia di alloro/foglia di lauro, bay leaf
foglia di vite, vine leaf
foiolo, tripe (stomach lining)
folpetto, the Venetian word for baby octopus
fondo di carciofo, artichoke heart
fonduta, melted cheese (fondue)
fontina, mild cheese (soft & creamy)
forchetta, fork
formaggini d'Alpe, cow's-milk cheese found in Ticino
formaggini di capra, fresh goat's-milk cheese found in Ticino
formaggio (formaggi), cheese
formaggio di fossa, aged sheep's-milk cheese
  from Le Marche
forno, al, baked
forte, strong
fracosta, rib steak
fragola (e), strawberry
fragole di bosco/fragoline di bosco, wild strawberries
fragolino, sea bream
fragolone, large strawberries
Frangelico, hazelnut-flavored cordial
frappé, milk shake
frascarelli, tiny *gnocchi*
Frascati, dry to slightly sweet white wine
frascota di bue, rib steak
frattaglie, giblets

foglia.

fragolone.

freddo (i)/fredda (e), cold/iced. *Tè freddo* is iced tea

fregolotta, flour, cornmeal & almond cake

fregula, dumpling soup

Freisa, dry to slightly sweet red wine

fresca (o), fresh/not cooked

freschi, wild mushrooms

Freschi –
FRESS-KEE

fresco, al, outside (in the fresh air)

fricando, round of veal

fricassea, fricassee

fricò, cheese pancake

friggere, deep-fried (to deep fry)

frittata, omelette

frittata casalinga, plain omelette

frittata semplice, plain omelette

frittatina di patate, potato omelette

frittella (e), pancake/fritter

fritti ascolani, mixed fry of lamb chops, brains, olives & zucchini

fritto (a)/fritti (e), fried/deep-fried

fritto alla milanese, breaded & deep-fried

fritto alla napoletana, deep-fried fish, cheese & vegetables

fritto alla romana, deep-fried sweetbreads

fritto di verdura, fried vegetables

fritto misto, mixed deep-fried fish, meat or vegetables

fritto misto alla Fiorentina, meat & vegetable fritters

frittura, frying/fry

frittura del paese, mixed floured & fried seafood

frittura di pesce, mixed dish of fried small fish, squid & shrimp

frizzante, semi-sparkling wine

frizzante.

frolla, tender (meat)/flaky pastry

frollini, biscuits

frullato, milk shake

frullato di frutta, fruit milk shake

frumento, wheat

frumentone, corn

frutta, fruit

frutta candita, candied fruit

frutta cotta, stewed fruit

frutta fresca, fresh fruit

frutta secca, dried fruit

frutti di bosco, berries

frutti di mare, seafood/seafood salad

fundador, w/brandy

funghetti, small mushroom-shaped pasta for soup

funghetto, al, sliced mushrooms cooked in garlic, onions & herbs

funghi trifolati, mushrooms sauteed in butter & garlic

fungo (funghi), mushroom

fuoco dell'Etna, strong, red Sicilian liquor

fusi, leg. *Fusi di pollo* is a chicken leg

fusilli, spiral-shaped pasta.

Fusilli corti are short & *fusilli lunghi* are long

fusto, shank

galatina (in gelatina), pressed meat in aspic

galantina tartufata, truffles in aspic jelly

galletta, cracker/cookie. Can also refer to a mushroom or grape

galletto, chicken (cock)

Galliano, herb liqueur (yellow in color)

gallina, chicken (hen)

gallinaccio, woodcock/chanterelle mushroom

gallina faraona, guinea fowl

gallinella, waterfowl

gallinella faraona, guinea fowl

gallo, John Dory fish in Sicily (a firm-textured, white-fleshed fish w/a mild, sweet flavor & low fat content)

gallo cedrone, grouse (a game bird)

gamba, leg/drumstick/shank

gamba di vitello, veal shank

gamberelli, shrimp

gamberetta di rana, frogs' legs

gamberetto (i), shrimp

gambero (i), lobster/crayfish/shrimp

gamberoni (gamberetti), large prawn

ganocchio, type of prawn

garetto, beef shank

garganelli, handmade pasta which is a square rolled into a tube (the dough is made from eggs, flour, grated *parmigiano* & nutmeg)

garofolato, beef stew

gaspaccio, gazpacho (the cold, tomato-based Spanish soup)

gasata/gassata, carbonated

galletto.

Gattinara, full-bodied red wine

gelatina, jelly/gelatine

gelato (i), ice cream/iced dessert

gelato al tartufo, ice cream w/chocolate sauce

gemelli, pasta made of two strands twisted around each other. The term means "twins"

genovese, alla, w/herbs (especially basil), olive oil & garlic/w/meat & onions

Genovese basil is considered the most fragrant.

germe di grano, wheat germ

germinus, almond-meringue cookies from Sardinia

germogli, sprouts

gesuita, rib steak

ghiacciato, chilled/iced

ghiaccio, ice

ghianchetti, small anchovies

ghiotta, alla, grilled or roasted

gesuito means Jesuit.. presumably because the priests got the best meat.

ghiozzo, mackerel

giallo d'uova, egg yolk

gianchetti, small anchovies

gianduia, chocolate & hazelnut ice cream

gianduiotti, hazelnut-and-chocolate candies

giambonette(i)/giambonetto, boned chicken roll w/filling

giardiniera, small pieces of vegetables (a garnish)

gigantoni, large tubular pasta (means "giant")

gioddu, yogurt in Sardinia

giorno, del, of the day

gin, gin *Good Guess!*

ginepro, juniper berry

ginestrata, chicken & sweet wine soup (a sweet & sour soup). A Tuscan specialty

girarrosto, spit-roasted

girasole, sunflower

girello, rump

glassate, glazed

girasole means turns to the sun.

gnoccata al pomodoro, tomato pizza

gnocchetti, small *gnocchi*

gnocchetti alla Sarda/gnocchetti sarda, small pasta dumplings in various sauces. A specialty in Sardinia

gnocchi, flour or potato dumplings

gnocchi alla marchigiana, *gnocchi* w/chicken-giblet sauce

gnocchi alla piemontese, little balls of flour, egg & potato

gnocchi alla romana, semolina (flour) dumplings

gnocchi di patate, little balls of potato, flour & egg

gnocco fritto, deep-fried rolls of pasta

gnocco ingrassato, *focaccia w/prosciutto*

gnudi, means naked (w/out pasta). Stuffing
only, such as in ***ravioli gnudi*** *gnudi... don't pronounce the G. NOO-DEE*

gnumariddi, a sweetbread dish

gomiti, "c"-shaped tubular pasta

gomma da masticare, chewing gum

gorgonzola, creamy, blue cheese (best-known Italian blue)

goulasch, goulash

graffo (i), doughnut *Kinda cute, hey?*

grana, mild, hard cheese (similar to *parmesan*)

granatina, steak tartare (raw ground beef). In most parts of
Italy this term means Italian ice or shaved ice

granceola, spider crab. A specialty of Venice

granchio (di mare), crab

granciporro (i), crab

grande, large

granello, seed

gran farro, grain & bean soup

grani di, seeds of...

granita, coffee or fruit syrup served over crushed ice
(a "snow cone"). Originally made from snow from Mt. Etna

grano, wheat/corn

grano duro, duram wheat

grano padano, buttery, hard, seasoned cheese
w/a grainy texture

grano saraceno, buckwheat

granoturco/granturco, corn on the cob

granseola, a crab found in Venice

grappa, liquor made from grape pressings.
It is extremely strong *Grappa is a popular digestivo which can taste like heaven... or hell.*

grappolo, a bunch
(as in a bunch of grapes)

grassi vegetali, vegetable oil

grasso (a), oily/fatty/fat/grease

graticola, grilled/broiled

gratin/gratinate, oven-browned w/cheese

gratinada, baked dish topped
w/grated cheese & breadcrumbs

gratis, free

grattugiato, grated

gratuito (a), free

gremolata, minced anchovies, parsely & lemon (used as a garnish)

grenadine, veal chunks (used in casserole dishes)

gricia, alla, w/bacon, onion, cheese & chili pepper

griglia, alla, grilled (usually charcoal grilled)

grigliata mista, mixed grill of meats or fish

Grignolino, high-quality red wine

grissino (i), long, thin bread stick

grongo, Conger eel

groppo, rump (meat)

groviera/groviera svizzera, sharp
cheese w/holes (like Swiss cheese)

guancia.

guancia, pig's cheek. *Al guanciale* means cooked w/bacon &
onions. Also refers to the delicacy of pig's cheek

guardaroba, coat room

guarnite, alla, served w/a garnish

guazzetto, usually refers to a stew (meat or fish). In Sardinia,
this dish almost always contains capers

gubana, sweet bread roll (dried fruit & nut strudel found in
Friuli-Venezia Giulia)

gulyas, beef stew found in Friuli-Venezia Giulia

gusti, flavors

hasce di manzo, hamburger patty

igname, yam

impanato (a), covered in breadcrumbs

impazzata di cozze/impepata di cozze, mussels cooked in
their own juice w/black pepper, oil, parsley & garlic

incapriata, purée of fava beans & chicory

incasciata, layered dough, meat sauce, hard-boiled eggs, cheese

incluso (a), included

Indiana, all', w/curry (Indian style)

indivia, endive/chicory

indivia Belga, Belgian endive

insaccati, salami

insalata, salad

insalata cotta...
Love it!

insalata all'americana, shrimp & mayonnaise salad

insalata caprese, tomatoes, basil & *mozzarella* salad.
Originally a specialty on the island of Capri, but now
found everywhere in Italy

insalata cotta, cold, cooked vegetable salad

insalata di campo, field lettuce

insalata di cesare, Caesar salad

insalata di crudita, mixed raw vegetable salad

insalata di frutti di mare, seafood salad

insalata di funghi, raw mushroom salad *not a favorite*

insalata di mare, seafood salad

insalata di patate, potato salad

insalata di petti di pollo, chicken salad w/walnuts

insalata di tonno, tuna salad

insalata di verdura cotta, boiled vegetable salad

insalata mista, mixed salad

insalata riccia, curly endive

insalata russa, diced potato & vegetable salad w/mayonnaise

insalata siciliana, salad featuring fennel & black olives

insalata verde, green salad

integrale, whole wheat

involtini al sugo, rolled veal cutlets w/ham & cheese & topped w/tomato sauce

involtini di cavolfiori, cabbage leaves stuffed w/meat

involtini di pesce, thin fish slices stuffed w/*prosciutto* & herbs

involtini di salvia, a deep-fried sage-leaf anchovy roll

involtini di vitello, veal roll usually stuffed w/salami & cheese

involtino (i), stuffed roll

iota, hearty vegetable soup (white beans, cabbage & bacon fat). A specialty of Trieste

Ischia, red & white wines from Southern Italy

I.V.A., abbreviation for Value Added Tax (V.A.T.)

jota, thick bean & sauerkraut soup (see Iota)

julienne, small strips of vegetables

kirsch, al, w/a clear cherry brandy

knoedel/knödeln, dumplings found in the Trentino-Alto Adige region *Krapfen... sounds good!*

krapfen, doughnuts (Austrian name)

laccetto, mackerel

lacerto, mackerel

Lacrima Christi, popular red, white & rosé wines *Lacrima Christi - tears of Christ*

Lago di Caldaro, light red wine

Lagrein Rosato, rosé wine

Lambrusco, well-known red wine (sweet)

lamelle di fegato, thin slices of liver sautéed in butter

lampasciuni, wild onions

lampone (i), raspberry
lampreda, lamprey
lanzado, mackerel
lardarellatta alla fiamma, larded & cooked on a grill
lardo, bacon/salt pork/lard
lardone, salt pork
lardoons, cured & fried pork
lardoso, meat fat
lasagne, thin layers of dough & meat, tomatoes, cheese & sauce (baked in the oven)
lasagne al forno, large strips of pasta cooked in sauce
lasagne alla portoghese, baked custard caramel
lasagne alla vincisgrassi, baked *lasagne* w/meatballs
lasagne verdi, spinach *lasagne*
latte, milk
latte al cacao, chocolate milk
latte di mandorla, almond milk
latte intero, whole milk
latte macchiato, steamed milk w/a small amount of *espresso.* Compare this to *espresso macchiato*
latte magro, skim milk
latterini, poached fish dish
latte scremato, skim milk
latticini, small *mozzarella* balls
lattonzolo, suckling pig
lattuga (e), lettuce
lattuga romana, romaine lettuce
lauro, bay leaf
lavarello, a type of salmon
laziale, alla, w/onions
lecca-lecca, sucker/lollypop
leccia, pompano
leggero, light or weak/light wine
legume (i), vegetable
lenticchia (e), lentil
lepre, rabbit/hare
lepre in salmì, marinated rabbit ("jugged rabbit")
leprotto, young rabbit
lessato (a), boiled
lesso, boiled. This can also refer to meat or fish stew
letterato, small tuna fish
lievito, yeast/baking powder

Lampreda. Non grazie!

Latte. generally not drunk by the glass.

lievito di birra, brewer's yeast

limonata, lemonade/lemon soda

limonata.

limoncello, alcohol & lemon-zest drink

limone (i), lemon. *Al limone* means w/lemon juice

lingua, tongue. This can also refer to sole (seafood)

linguine, flat noodles

liquore (i), liqueur. *Liquore Strega* is a sweet herb liqueur

liquoroso, fortified dessert wine

liscia/lisce, refers to smooth pasta (w/out ridges)

liscio, straight. *Brodo liscio* is plain broth

lissa, pompano in Venice

lista, menu

lista dei vini, wine list

livornese, alla, usually beans in tomato sauce
   w/celery & onions

locale, local

lodigiano, a type of *parmesan* cheese

Lombarda, alla, served fried in butter w/lemon juice & parsley

lombata, loin/leg. *Lombata di maiale* is a pork chop. *Lombata
   di vitello* is a grilled veal chop

lombata ai sassi, floured steak sautéed in butter w/sage & fried
   potatoes

lombatine, tenderloin or cut of meat for filet mignon

lombello, loin/leg

lombo di manzo, beef loin/sirloin

lombo di vitello, veal sirloin

lonza, loin

lucanica, spicy sausage

lucerna (e), grouper

luccio, pike

Lumaca.

lucullo, alla, raw beef (steak tartare)

Lugana, dry white wine

luganega, pork sausage. This spicy sausage from Basilicata
   has many similar spellings such as *luganica* & *lucanica*

lumaca (lumache), snail. *Lumache* also refers to snail-shaped
   pasta. *Lumachine* is a small version of this pasta
   used in soup

lumache alla Bourguignonne, snails w/garlic butter
   ("Burgundy snails")

lunga, long (as in long pasta or *pasta lunga*)

lungo, lighter *espresso*

lupo di mare, sea perch

luvasu, sea bream
maccarello, mackerel
maccarones con bottarga, Sardinian pasta w/fish eggs
maccaruni di casa, Sicilian pasta dish served
    w/tomato & meat sauce
maccheroni, *macaroni*
maccheroni al pettine, pasta w/ridges usually served w/ragù
macchiato, coffee or *espresso* w/milk
macco di fave, broad bean, onion & tomato soup
macedonia di frutta, fruit salad
macedonia di legumi, mixed cooked vegetables
macinata, ground. *La carne macinata* is ground beef
madera, al, cooked in Madeira wine
mafaldine, pasta ribbons
maggiorana, marjoram
magro, dish w/no meat/lean.
    Ravioli di magro is stuffed pasta
    w/herbs & *ricotta* cheese
maiale, pork
maionese, mayonnaise
mais, corn

marjoram is a member of the oregano family.

malfatti di ricotta, *ricotta gnocchi. Malfatti* means badly
    made, a reference to the handmade dumplings in this dish
malloreddus, flavored dumplings found in Sardinia
malloreddus all'oristanese, saffron-flavored dumplings w/a
    sauce of Swiss chard, cream & eggs
maltagliata, *macaroni*
mammole, artichokes

mammole.

mancia, tip
mandarino (i), tangerine/mandarin
mandorla (e)/mandorlata, almond
manicotti, stuffed (w/cheese & meats), baked pasta dish
mantecato, whipped ice cream. This also refers to a way to
    prepare cod
manzo (di bue), beef
manzo arrosto ripieno, stuffed roast
manzo lesso, boiled beef
manzo salato, corned beef
manzo stufato al vino rosso, beef stewed in red wine
maraschino/marasco, w/Maraschino (cherry-flavored liqueur)
marchigiana, alla, a dish in the style of Le Marche (one of the
    regions of Italy), usually cooked w/chicken giblet sauce

mare, di, of the sea

mare-monti, a dish served w/mushrooms & shrimp

margarina, margarine

margherita, this term is used to describe a pizza w/tomato, *mozzarella* & basil

marinara, alla, usually, but not always, means in tomato sauce (usually w/garlic & onions). The term means "of the sea" or "sailor's style," so can also refer to a dish w/seafood

marinata (o), marinated

maritozzo, soft bread roll

marmellata, marmalade/jam

marmellata d'arance, marmalade

marrone (i), chestnut. *Marrons glaces* are candied chestnuts

Marsala, fortified dessert wine from Sicily

marsala, al, in a Marsala (fortified dessert wine) sauce

Martini, vermouth

mascarpone, a soft, very creamy, fresh cheese (even for cheese, it is high fat)

masenette, tiny crabs eaten whole (w/the shell)/Venetian word for small soft-shelled crabs

matriciana, bacon, tomato & spices sauce

mattone, al, pounded flat (usually chicken) & roasted in a brick oven

mazza da tamburo, a parasol-shaped mushroom

mazzancelle/mazzancolle, very large prawns

mazzancougni, very large prawns

medaglione, medallions

medallione, a grilled ham & cheese sandwich

media, medium

mela (e), apple

melacotogna, quince

melagrana, pomegranate

melanzana (e), eggplant

eggplant is a member of the same family as tomatoes, potatoes & peppers.

melanzane al funghetto, sautéed eggplant

melanzane alla Napoletana, eggplant Neopolitan style (layered w/cheese & tomato puree & baked in an oven)

melanzane alla parmigiana, eggplant *parmesan* (w/tomatoes & *parmesan* cheese)

melanzane ripiene, stuffed eggplant

melassa, molasses

meliga, cornmeal

melone, melon/canteloupe

menta, mint
mentine, mints
menù, menu
menù a prezzo fisso, set menu
menù turistico, fixed-price menu
merca, roast fish dish from Sardinia
merenda, late morning/afternoon snack
meringa, meringue
meringa chantilly, meringue shells filled w/whipped cream
meringato/meringhe/meringua, meringue
merlango, hake/cod/whiting
merlano, whiting, cod or hake
merluzzo, cod
messicani, veal scallops dish/veal rolls
mesticanza, mixture of salad greens
metà, half
mezzo (a), half
mezzelune ai pinoli, pine-nut cookies from Umbria
mezze maniche, short tubular pasta
miascia, bread & fruit pudding
midollo, marrow
miele, honey   *millefoglie means*
miglio, millet   *a thousand leaves*
milanese, alla, battered w/eggs & breadcrumbs & fried
Millefiori, herb-based liqueur
millefoglie, puff pastry/napoleon
millerighe, ridged tubular pasta (means "thousand lines"
    after the ridges in the pasta)
mimosa, spongecake & whipped-cream dessert
minerale, mineral (as in *acqua minerale* or mineral water)
minestra (minestre), soup (usually thick soup)
minestra al farro, soup made from the grain
    emmer (a hard red wheat)
minestra di cipolle, onion soup
minestra di fagioli, bean soup
minestra di farina tostata, toasted-flour soup
minestra di farro, "spelt" soup. Wheat (spelt) soup w/ ham bone
minestra di funghi, cream of mushroom soup
minestra di lenticchie, lentil soup
minestra di pomodoro, tomato soup
minestra di riso, rice soup
minestra in brodo, broth w/noodles or rice & chicken livers

minestra maritata, meat broth & vegetable soup
minestre di piscialetto, dandelion-greens soup
minestrina, soup (usually clear)
minestrone, bean & vegetable soup w/noodles, vegetables, rice
minestrone alla genovese, vegetable soup
   w/*macaroni* & spinach
minestrone verde, thick vegetable soup w/herbs & beans
mirabella (e), small plum
mirtillo (i), blueberry. The word *mirtilli* is also used for berries
   in general & for cranberries
mischianza, salad of wild greens, herbs & edible flowers
misoltini, salted & dried shad (fish)
misticanza, salad of wild greens, herbs & edible flowers
misto/misti, mixed
misto del golfo/misto del paese, mixed floured & fried seafood
misto mare, mixed floured & fried seafood
mitilo, mussel
moka, mocha
molto, very
montanara, alla, has many meanings but generally means
   w/red wine sauce or w/vegetables
montare, to whip (usually refers to cream)
montebianco/Mont Blanc, pyramid of sweetened chestnuts &
   whipped cream (named after Mont Blanc) *Mont Blanc*
Montepulciano, full-bodied, dry red wine *is the*
montone, mutton *French side of*
monzittas, snails in Sardinia *Monte Bianco*
mora (e), blackberry *mountain.*
mormora, small fish found in the Mediterranean
mortadella, luncheon meat w/pistachio nuts & peppercorns
morto, pot roast
mosca, con la, a drink (usually *Sambuca*) served "w/the
   fly"(*con la mosca*). The "fly" is a coffee bean in the glass
moscardino (i), small squid
Moscatello/Moscato, muscatel (table & dessert white & red
   wines from the muscat grape)
mostarda, mustard. This word is rarely used. Most use *senape*
mostarda di frutta, candied fruits in syrup/preserved fruits in
   a mustard sauce/fruit chutney
mousse al cioccolato, chocolate mousse
mozzarella, a soft, fresh (unripened), slightly sweet cheese
mozzarella di bufala, *mozzarella* made from buffalo milk

mozzarella in carrozza, fried *mozzarella* sandwich
   (means "in a carriage")
muddica, breadcrumbs in Sicily
muggine, grey mullet
muscoletti, shank
muscoli, mussels. This word is rarely used. Most use *cozze*
muscoli alla marinara, steamed mussels dish
musetto, salami
napoletana, ("Naples-style") w/tomato sauce (w/out meat)
nasello, whiting/hake/cod
naturale, plain/natural
nave, di, w/seafood
navone (i), turnip
`nduja, Calabrian pork sausage
Nebbiolo, full-bodied dry red wine
nepitella, an herb similar to mint
nero (a), black
nervetti, calf's foot dish (tendons of calves' feet).
   A Venetian specialty
nespola, medlar (a tart fruit)
nidi di rondine, pasta rolls
nocciola (e), hazelnut
noccioline americane, peanuts
nocciole, nuts
noce (i), nut/walnut. Can also refer to the top round of veal
noce di cocco, coconut
nocelli, walnut-raisin cookies
noce moscata, nutmeg
nocepesca, nectarine
noci d'anacardo, cashews
Nocillo/Nocino, liquor made from walnuts
nodino (i), chop/small grilled pork chop
non, not
non fumatori, no smoking
non gassata, still or not carbonated
nonna, alla, this can be any sauce served w/pasta. The term
   means "grandmother" & there are as many variations of
   "alla nonna" as there are grandmothers
norcina, sausage & cheese sauce. After the town of Norcia
Norma, alla, this usually refers to a dish served w/eggplants,
   tomatoes, basil & sometimes *ricotta* cheese
nostrale/nostrano, home-grown/local

Navone.

nervetti...
I don't
think so.

novellame, a spread of salted anchovies & *peperoncino* sauce
novello/novelli, fresh/tender
o, or
oca, goose
occhiate, orata (a fish)
occhi di lupo, small tubular pasta
   "wolves' eyes")
olio, oil/olive oil
olio d'arachide, peanut oil
olio da tavola, salad oil
olio di cartamo, safflower oil
olio di girasole, sunflower oil
olio di grano/olio di granturco, corn oil
olio di palma, palm oil
olio di semi, seed oil/corn oil
olio d'oliva, olive oil
olio santo, chili-infused oil
oliva (e), olive (*nere*, black, *verdi,* green)
olive agrodolci, olives in sugar & vinegar
olive ascolane, large green olives. *Olive all'ascolana*,
   in Le Marche, olives are stuffed meat & fried in olive oil
ombra, glass of wine in Venice. This word is usually used at a
   bar & not at a restaurant
ombrina, umbrine (seafood/bass)
omelette, omelette
omelette casalinga, plain omelette
omelette semplice, plain omelette
oranciata, orangeade
orata, a fish found in the Mediterranean (porgy)
oratino, a small *orata* fish
orecchiette, small ear-shaped pasta
orecchiette con le cime di rapa, small ear-shaped pasta
   w/turnips. A specialty in Apulia
origano, oregano
ortaggi, vegetables/greens/herbs
Orvieto, light, dry, white wine from Orvieto in Umbria
orzata, almond or barley-flavored water
orzetto, barley & potato soup
orzo (i), rice-shaped pasta. Can also refer to barley
osso, bone
ossobuco (ossibuchi), braised veal-shank dish. You may be
   given a marrow spoon to eat the marrow in the bone

Olio d'oliva
we never leave
Italy without
a bottle.

ossobuco alla milanese, veal shank, tomatoes, garlic & wine

ostrica (ostriche), oyster

ovalina, a type of *mozzarella* cheese

ovolo (i), a rare (& delicious) mushroom w/an orange & scarlet color. Sometimes called Caesar's mushroom

pacchetto, package

paciugo, parfait

padella, in, fried

paesana, alla, usually means served w/bacon (or sausage), potatoes, carrots & other vegetables

paeta, spit-roasted turkey

pagaro/pagello, sea bream/porgy

paglia e fieno, pasta dish w/yellow (egg) & green (spinach) pasta (means "straw & hay")

pagliarino, soft, mild cheese

pagliata, a dish containing organ meat

pagnotta, loaf

pagnotta del cacciatore, game birds roasted in dough

pagro, sea bream/porgy

paiata, spit-roasted turkey

paillard, beef rib steak or veal cutlet pounded thin & grilled

pajata, a dish containing organ meat

palamito, bonito fish

palemone, prawns

pallina, scoop (as in scoop of ice cream). The word really means "marble"

palomba/palombaccia, pigeon

palombacci, an Umbrian dish of small birds cooked whole on a spit

palombo, dogfish/shark found in Sicily

panafittas, dried bread broken into pieces & boiled (like pasta), then served in a tomato sauce in Sardinia

panardo, a thirty-course feast served in Abruzzo

panata, bread soup

pancetta, bacon (cured pork belly)

pancetta arrotolata, rolled bacon flavored w/cloves

pan có Santi, sweet bread w/raisins, dates, honey & walnuts. "Saints' bread" is eaten around All Saints Day (November 1)

pan di Genova, almond cake

palomba.

They're all over the damn place.

pan di Spagna, spongecake

pandolce, cake w/dried fruit

pandoro (di Verona), star-shaped light cake w/sugar topping

pane, bread/loaf

pane bianco, white bread

pane bigio, whole-wheat bread

pane carasau, flat crispy bread found in Sardinia. Also known as *carta da musica* (music paper)

pane di segale, rye bread

pane e coperto, the charge for bread & for sitting at the table

pane frattau, *pane carasau* topped w/tomato sauce, grated cheese & a fried egg. A specialty in Sardinia

pane grattugiato, breadcrumbs

pane integrale, whole-wheat bread

panelle, chickpea fritters

pane nero, dark bread

pane pepato, gingerbread

pane piccante, gingerbread

pane scuro, pumpernickel bread

pane toscano, sourdough bread

pane tostato, toast

panettone, spiced cakes or coffeecakes w/candied fruits

panforte, flat, hard fruitcake

pan grattato, breadcrumbs

Pane.
the Italians,
like the French,
are fiercely
proud of their
bread.

panicielli d'uva passula, grapes wrapped in leaves & baked

panino (i), roll/sandwich

panino imbottito, sandwich

paniscia, rice, sausage & bean soup

pan matteloch, honey bread found in the lake country

pan meino, cornmeal bread/cake (millet bread) w/elderflowers

panna, cream

panna, alla, served in a cream sauce or w/creamy gravy

panna, con, in a cream sauce/w/cream

panna cotta, rich cream custard

panna da montare/panna montata, whipped cream

pannocchia, corn on the cob

panpepato, gingerbread or hazelnut cake

pansoti/pansotti, triangular-shaped filled pasta

pan tostato, toast

panzanella, bread & vegetable salad

panzerotti, baked (or deep-fried) dough filled w/pork, cheese, tomatoes or other ingredients

panzoni, stuffed ravioli dish

paparot, cornmeal & spinach dish from Friuli-Venezia Giulia

pappa al pomodoro, tomato & bread soup

pappardelle, long, flat, wide pasta

pappardelle al sugo di lepre/pappardelle alla lepre, strips of
  pasta w/rabbit sauce

paprica, paprika

pardulas, Sardinian pastries filled w/cream cheese

parigina, hamburger buns. In Sicily, this refers to bread

parmigiana, alla, w/*parmesan* cheese & tomatoes

parmigiana di melanzane, baked slices of eggplant layered
  w/*parmesan* cheese, tomatoes & *mozzarella*

parmigiano, *parmesan* cheese usually served grated

parmigiano-reggiano, the "real" name for *parmesan* cheese

partenopea, means "Naples' style," the same as *Napolitana*

Pasqualina, "Easter style" which can mean roasted in an oven
  w/olive oil, onion, garlic, black olives & celery. *Torta
  Pasqualina* is a pie featuring artichokes

passate di legumi, puree of vegetables

passatelli, pasta of *parmesan* cheese, eggs & breadcrumbs

passato, puree

passato di verdura, cream of vegetable soup

passera di mare, flounder

passera pianuzza, flounder

passerino, flounder

pasta, pasta (dough made of
  flour, oil, butter, eggs & water).
  The first course in Italy. If you find
  -ette or *-ini* after pasta, this means a smaller version of
  pasta. For example, *pennette & pennini* are smaller versions
  of *penne.* If you find *-oni* after pasta, this means a large
  pasta like *rigatoni. Pasta* that starts w/*taglia* is made of long,
  thin strips. *Pasta* can also mean pastry

pasta al forno, any pasta mixed w/a sauce & baked

pasta alla Norma, pasta w/tomatoes, basil & eggplant topped
  w/*ricotta* cheese

pasta asciutta, any pasta not eaten in soup

pasta con le sarde, pasta w/fresh sardines

pasta d'arachide, peanut butter

pasta di olive, olive paste

pasta e ceci, pasta & chickpea soup

*passera
di
mare*

pasta e fagioli, pasta & bean soup
pasta frolla, puff pastry
pasta in brodo, pasta in broth
pasta 'ncasciata, pasta baked w/eggplant, salami, tomato/basil
pasta reale (paste reali), marzipan cake (means "royal pastry")
pasta sfoglia, puff-pastry dough
paste, pastries
pastella, batter for frying
pasticceria (e), pastry
pasticcetti, small tarts
pasticciata, baked pasta (in a casserole)
pasticcini da te, teacakes/small pastries
pasticcino (i), cake/small pastry/tart
pasticcio, pastry/pie. Also the Venetian word for baked lasagne
pasticcio di maccheroni, sweet pie containing meat sauce
pastiera napoletana, *ricotta* cheese-filled pastry
pastina, small pasta usually used in soup
pastina in brodo, pasta served in soup
pastissa, pot pie
pasto, meal
patata (e), potato
patate al lesso, boiled potatoes

Anti-before
pasto-meal
antipasto.

patate al ghiotto/patate alla ghiottona, stuffed baked potatoes
patate americane, sweet potato
patate arroste, roasted potatoes
patate bollite, boiled potatoes
patate dolci, sweet potato
patate fritte, fried potatoes/french fries
patate in padella, potatoes fried in a pan
patate lesse, boiled potatoes
patate novelle, new potatoes
patate rosolate, roasted potatoes
patate saltate, potatoes sliced & sautéed
patate tenere, new potatoes
patatine fritte, french fries/chips
patatine novelle, small roasted potatoes
pate/paterini, pâté
pecora, sheep/ewe
pecorino, hard, sharp cheese usually served grated. ***Pecorino alla griglia*** is a Sardinian specialty of grilled *pecorino* cheese
pellegrine, scallops

penne, tube-shaped pasta (cut at an angle)

pennette, smaller version of *penne*

penneziti, larger version of *penne*

pennoni, the largest version of *penne*

peoci, mussels. Also the Venetian word for "head lice"

pepata di cozze, mussels in a black pepper, oil & garlic sauce

pepato, peppered

pepe, black pepper

pepe di Giamaica, allspice

peperonata, tomatoes, peppers & onion stewed together

peperoncino (i), small, spicy pickled pepper

peperone (i), pepper

peperoni alla brace, roasted marinated peppers

peperoni imbottiti, stuffed peppers

peperoni ripieni, stuffed peppers

peperoni rossi, red peppers

peperoni sott'aceto, pickled chilis

peperoni verdi, green peppers

pera (e), pear

perciatelli, hollow spaghetti noodles

per contorno, meal includes salad or side dish

pere helene/pere elena, poached pear served in vanilla ice cream & topped w/chocolate sauce

pernice, partridge

persico, perch

pesca (pesche), peach

pesca melba, peaches in syrup w/ice cream & whipped cream

pescatora/pescatore, seafood sauce for pasta & rice dishes

pescatrice, angler fish

pesce, fish

pesce carpionata, marinated fish in herbs

pesce in saor, fish in a sauce of onion, raisin, pine nut & vinegar. A specialty in Veneto

pesce persico, perch

pesce San Pietro, John Dory fish (a firm-textured, white-fleshed fish w/a mild, sweet flavor and low fat content)

pesce sciabola, an eel-like fish

pesce serra, bluefish

pesce spada, swordfish

pesce stocco, cod

pesce turchino, mackerel

pesche, peaches

pesche aurora, spongecake soaked in peach liqueur

pesto, basil, oil, garlic & pine-nut sauce

petonchio, scallops

petroniana, alla, can mean many things, most frequently breaded & fried & topped w/melted cheese

pettine (i), small scallop

petto, breast (of poultry)

petto alla principessa, chicken floured & fried in butter & served w/an egg on top

petto all'arancio, chicken in an orange sauce

petto di pollo, chicken breast

peverada, chicken liver & anchovy sauce *only for the brave.*

pezzenta, pork salami

pezzo, piece

piacere, of your own choice (your pleasure)

piadina, soft, flat bread

pianuzza, flounder/halibut

piastra, grilled on a flat steel plate

piattino, saucer

piatto (i), dish/plate. *Piatti freddi* means cold dishes

piatto del giorno, dish of the day

piccante, highly seasoned (hot)

piccata (e), veal scallop

piccata all'allegro, veal scallop fried in butter w/lemon juice

piccata alla Lombarda, veal scallop fried in butter w/lemon juice & parsley

piccata di vitello, veal cooked in lemon & parsley

piccatina, veal scallop dish

piccioncino, young pigeon

piccione, pigeon

piccione selvatico, wild pigeon

piccolo (i)/piccola (e), small

pici, eggless pasta

piede (i), foot

piemontese, sauce w/truffles ("Piedmont style")

pietanza, dish/main course

pignata, lamb or goat w/herbs. A specialty from Basilicata named after the terra-cotta pot it is cooked in

pimento, pimento/allspice

pimiento, sweet red peppers

pinoccate/pinocchiata, almond & pine-nut cake

pinolata, pine-nut dessert cake found in Tuscany

pinolo (i), pine nut

Pinot Grigio, light, fruity white wine

pinsimonio/pinzimonio, oil, pepper & salt dressing/oil &
  mustard dressing for dipping

pinza, yellow flour, pine nut & raisin cake from Veneto

pipe, pasta similar to *lumache* (a snail-shaped pasta)

pisello (i), pea

pistacchi, pistachio nuts

pitta, pizza either stuffed or
  topped with many ingredients.
  Popular in Calabria

piviere, plover (bird)

pizza, pizza

pizza alla marinara, the "true"
  pizza: tomato, olive oil & oregano

Pizza... Man's highest culinary achievement.

pizza alla napoletana, pizza w/cheese, capers, tomatoes,
  anchovies, olives & *mozzarella*

pizza alla siciliana, pizza w/salami or ham, anchovies, olives,
  tomatoes & *mozzarella*

pizza bianca, pizza bread topped w/sea salt & olive oil

pizza capricciosa, same as *pizza quattro stagioni*

pizza di Pasqua, cheese bread

pizzaiola, w/tomato & garlic sauce

pizzaiolo, pizza man (the maker of pizzas)

pizza margherita, pizza w/tomato, basil & *mozzarella*

pizza marinara, pizza w/garlic, oil & oregano. Can also refer
  to a pizza w/black olives, anchovies, tomatoes & capers

pizza quattro stagioni, w/seafood, cheese,
  artichokes & ham in four sections.
  Means "four seasons" & is a pizza which has a
  different topping for each quarter

pizza rustica, common in central Italy; serves large rectangular
  pizzas with thicker crusts and more toppings than usually
  found in a *pizzeria*. You can order as much as you want, and
  pay by weight

pizzelle, small (fried) pizzas

pizzetta, small pizza

pizzoccheri, pasta made w/buckwheat flour

polenta, cornmeal mush

polenta concia, *polenta* w/cheese

polenta di grano saraceno, buckwheat *polenta*

polenta dolce, sweet *polenta* dessert

polenta e osei, *polenta* w/roast fowl

polenta grassa, butter, fontina cheese & *polenta*

polenta pasticciata, *polenta* served w/meat sauce, cheese, mushrooms & sauce (*polenta* pie)

polipetto (i), small squid/baby octopus

polipo (i)/polpo (i), octopus

pollame, poultry

pollastra/pollastrello, young chicken

pollo al mattone is a favorite!

pollo al mattone/pollastrino al mattone, chicken pounded flat & roasted in a brick oven

polletto, spring chicken

pollo, chicken

pollo alla diavola, highly spiced, grilled chicken

pollo alla Marengo, sautéed chicken dish with many ingredients (usually tomatoes, mushrooms & onions). The dish takes its name from the town of Marengo, where Napoleon defeated the Austrians

pollo alla Romana, fried chicken pieces, bacon & garlic

pollo all'arrabbiata, "Enraged chicken" (a spicy chicken dish)

pollo arrosto, roasted chicken

pollo fritto Fiorentina, chicken marinated in oil, lemon juice & herbs

pollo in bellavista, roasted chicken dish w/vegetables

pollo novello, spring chicken

pollo piccata al Marsala, chicken pounded thin & fried in butter & Marsala wine

pollo scarpariello, boneless chicken w/lemon, garlic & parsley

polpa, lean meat/flesh

polpetielle, baby octopus

polpetta (e) di carne, meatball

polpetti affogati, small octopuses cooked w/tomatoes (means "drowned octopuses")

polpettine (i), meatball. *Polpettine di pesce* is a seafood ball

polpettone, meat loaf

polpi arricciati, "curled octopus." An octopus dish in which the octopus is curled by beating & twirling it in a basket

polpo, octopus

polpo in purgatorio, octopus sautéed in oil w/tomatoes & peppers

pomi d'oro, the original name for tomato (means "golden apple"). It is believed that the tomato arrived in Europe w/a golden color that turned red under the hot Mediterranean sun

pommarola (salsa di), tomato sauce
pomo (i), apple
pomodoro (i), tomato
pomodoro, al, w/tomato sauce
pomodoro doppio (concentrato), thick tomato paste
pomodoro pelati, peeled tomatoes in their own juice
pomodoro pumate, sun-dried tomato
pomodoro super cirio, thick tomato pureé
pomodori con tonno, tomatoes stuffed w/tuna
pomodori secchi, sun-dried tomatoes
pompelmo, grapefruit
popone, melon
porcecellino, suckling pig
porceddu/porcheddu, Sardinian word for roast suckling pig
porcello, young pig
porchetta, roast suckling pig stuffed w/herbs
porcini, mushrooms (the wild mushroom boletus)
porco, pork
porri dorati, battered & deep-fried leeks
porro (i), leek
portacenere, ashtray
portafoglio, veal cutlet stuffed
   w/herbs, cheese & other ingredients.
   This is also the word for wallet
portata (e), course
porto, port
portoghese, usually means
   w/tomato sauce
porzione, portion
posillipo, seafood sauce
praio, dorade (fish)/gilt-head bream
pranzo, lunch/dinner
presnitz, dessert made w/dried fruit from
   Fruili-Venezia Giulia
prezzemolo (i), parsley
prezzo, price
prezzo fisso, fixed price
prima colazione, breakfast
primavera, spring vegetables & cream sauce
primizie, spring vegetables or fruit
primo, first (as in *primo piatto*, first course)
principale, main (as in *piatto principale*, main course)

porta cenere
Can't get
away from
it in Italy.

profiterole, filled ice-cream puff topped w/chocolate sauce & whipped cream

prosciutto, aged & cured ham

prosciutto affumicato, cured, smoked ham

prosciutto cotto, cooked or boiled ham

prosciutto crudo, salted, cured ham/Parma ham

prosciutto di cinghiale, smoked wild boar

prosciutto di San Daniele, a cured ham
    named after a town in the Friuli-Venezia Giulia region

prosciutto e melone, ham & melon

prosciutto di Parma, Parma ham
    (famous cured ham of Parma)

Prosecco, sparkling white wine from Veneto

provatura, soft, mild & sweet cheese

provenzale, onions, black olives, tomato & mushroom sauce

provolone, mild buffalo cheese

provolone dolce, mild, white, medium-hard cheese

provolone piccante, sharp cheese

prugna (e), plum

prugna secca (prugne secche), prune

pumaruolo/pumaruoro, tomato in Sicily & Campania

pumate, sun-dried tomatoes

punta di vitello, veal brisket

puntarelle, a salad green

punte di asparagi, asparagus tips

Punt e Mes, orange-flavored vermouth
    (drunk before meals)

puntino, a, medium done

punto, breast. *Punto* also means medium rare

purea, pureed/mashed

purea di fave, a puree of broad beans
    often spread on bread

purè di patate, mashed potatoes

puttanaio, a stew-like ratatouille
    (means "prostitute stew")

Absolute favorite

puttanesca, tomato, black olives, capers & garlic sauce (the term means "prostitute"). Allegedly named because prostitutes could prepare this quick meal between "customers"

quadrello, pork loin

quadrello d'agnello, rack of lamb

quadretti, refers to small squares of pasta

quadrucci, square-shaped pasta for soup

quaglia (e), quail

quattro formaggi, four cheeses

quattro spezie, four spices combined
 (pepper, cloves, juniper & nutmeg)

quattro stagioni, pizza
 w/seafood, cheese,
 artichokes & ham
 in four sections

Quattro Stagione means Four Seasons

rabarbaro, rhubarb. This can also refer to an
 after-dinner liqueur

radiatori, pasta shaped like a radiator

radicchio, red endive/red chicory (bitter red lettuce)

rafano, horseradish

ragnetto, rolls

ragno, sea bass

ragno di mare, spider crab

ragù, tomato-based meat sauce

ragusano, hard, slightly sweet cheese

ramolaccio, horseradish

ranapescatrice, angler fish

rane, frogs or frogs' legs

rannocchi, frog or frogs' legs

rapa (e), turnip

rape rosse, beet root

raspante, farm-raised (usually chicken). Means "scratching"

Ratafia, black-cherry liqueur

rattatuia, ratatouille

ravanada, horseradish sauce

ravanello (i), radish

raviggiolo, goat's-milk cheese

ravioli, squares of pasta w/stuffing. *Raviolini* are half-circle
 stuffed pasta

ravioli gnudi, ravioli stuffing (without the pasta)

ravioli verdi, spinach ravioli

razza, ray

recchie/recchietelle, the word in Apulia for *orecchiette* (ear-
 shaped pasta)

remolazzitt, radish

rene (i), kidney

ribes, currants

ribes neri, black currants

Rana.

ribes rossi, red currants

ribollita, vegetable soup (which means "reboiled") thickened w/bread. There are many versions of this Tuscan soup

ricciarelli, marzipan &/or almond biscuits

riccio (di mare)/ricci (di mare), sea urchin

ricciola, amberjack (fish)

riccioli, small, curly pasta

riccolo, curly endive

ricotta, similar to cottage cheese, sweetened when used in desserts

ricotta al maraschino, *ricotta* cheese w/maraschino

rigaglia (e), giblets

rigata (e), refers to ridges in pasta

rigatoni, large tube-shaped pasta (always has ridges)

rigatoni alla Norma, a Sicilian dish of pasta w/eggplant & tomato sauce

righini, bluegill

ripieno/ripiene, stuffed

riserva, mature wine

risi e bisi, creamy rice w/green peas. *Bisi* is the Venetian word for peas

riso (i), rice

riso ai gamberi, rice w/shrimp

riso alla genovese, rice w/sauce of minced beef (or veal) w/vegetables

riso alla Greca, rice, vegetables & sausage dish (Greek style)

riso alla milanese, golden rice dish from Milan featuring saffron

riso alla pilota, rice w/a sausage meat sauce

riso e ceci, broth of rice & chickpeas w/tomatoes & spices

riso in bianco, white rice w/butter

riso in cagnone, boiled rice topped w/*parmesan* cheese

riso mantecado, rice cooked in butter & milk

riso nero, black rice. The rice is made black from squid ink

risoni, rice-shaped pasta for soup

risotto, creamy rice dish w/various ingredients. Served as a first course, *i primi,* after the *antipasto*

risotto ai fiori di zucca, rice dish made w/a heavy cream base & zucchini flowers stirred in w/*parmesan*. A Ticino specialty

risotto alla certosina, creamy rice dish w/shrimp, mushrooms, peas & sometimes frogs' legs

risotto alla mantovana, rice dish w/salami & *parmesan* cheese

Ribollita means Reboiled.

Risi e Bisi... another favorite.

risotto alla milanese, rice w/butter, saffron, beef, zucchini & *parmesan*

risotto alla pescatora, spicy rice w/seafood

risotto alla romana, rice usually w/lamb & potatoes

risotto alla valdostana, rice w/cheese & wine

risotto alla Valenciana, the same dish as Spanish *paella*

risotto alla Veneta, rice w/mussels

risotto alla veronese, rice & ham w/mushrooms

risotto al salto, crisp rice cake

risotto di frutti di mare, rice w/shellfish

risotto di peoci, rice w/mussels

risotto nero, black *risotto.*
Squid or cuttlefish ink makes the rice black

ristretto, reduced broth

robiola, soft, mild & slightly sweet cheese

robiolina, sheep's-milk cheese

rocciate, pastry w/fruit & nuts

rognoncini, kidneys

rognoncini al vino bianco, kidneys in white-wine sauce

rognone (i), kidney

rolatine di vitello, veal cutlets stuffed w/ham &/or cheese

rollè, roll

romagnola, usually means tomato, garlic & parsley sauce, but can mean many other things

romana, alla, a seasoned meat sauce w/any number of other ingredients

rombo, turbot

rosato, rosé

rosbif, roast beef

roscioli, red mullet in Abruzzo

rosé, rosé (blush) wine

rosmarino, rosemary

Rosolio, sweet liqueur

rospo, monkfish/angler fish. *Rospo* also means toad, so this fish is often referred to as *pesce rospo*

rosso, red

Rosso Antico, cherry-flavored vermouth

rotella, round

rotelle/rotelline, wheel-shaped pasta

rotolo, rolled meat w/stuffing.
Rotolo di spinaci is a spinach roll (pasta w/spinach)

rovi, blackberries

rucola, arugula, also called rocket salad

rughetta, salad green

rujolos, Sardinian sweet-cheese fritters

rum, rum

ruote di carro, pasta in the shape of a wheel (same as *rotelle*)

rustica, alla, usually means a pepper & olive sauce, but can mean many things

sagro, sea bream

salame (i), smoked sausage. *Salamino* is a small salami

salame di cioccolato/ salame al cioccolato, chocolate cake in the shape of (& looks like) a salami

salamino piccante, pepperoni

salatina, greens for salad

salatini, crackers/snacks

salato, salted/salami

salciccia, sausage

sale, salt

salmi, in, marinated in wine, garlic & herbs (usually w/game)

salmone, salmon. *Salmoncino* is young salmon

salsa, sauce

salsa bianca, white sauce

salsa di pommarola, tomato sauce

salsa di salsiccie, sausage sauce

salsa per la cacciagione, "hunters' sauce" for cooking game

salsa tartara, tartar sauce

salsa verde, parsley-based green sauce (w/oil, lemon juice, capers & garlic)

salsicce di maiale, pork sausages

salsiccia (e), fresh sausage

saltato (i)/saltata (e), sautéed

saltimbocca, veal cutlet wrapped around ham & sage

salumi, sausages

salumi cotti, cooked sausages & cured meats

salvia, sage

salvietta, napkin (paper)

Sambuca, anise-flavored liqueur. When served *con la mosca* ("w/the fly"), the "fly" is a coffee bean in the glass

sanato, young calf

sandwich, sandwich

Sangiovese, dry red wine from Emilia-Romagna

sangue, al, rare

handwritten: Salame!

handwritten: Saltimbocca means jump in the mouth.

Sanguinaccio, blood sausage (black pudding).
Also a chocolate spread made from chocolate & pigs' blood

San Pietro, John Dory fish (a firm-textured, white-fleshed fish
w/a mild, sweet flavor and low fat content)

San Severo, dry red wine from southern Italy

saor, sweet & sour sauce

sapa, thick sauce made from the juice of freshly pressed grapes

saporito (a), mild/tasty

sarago (saraghi), bluegill

Sarde.

sarda (e)/sardine, sardine

sarda, alla, tomato & meat sauce w/herbs & red wine
("Sardinian style")

sarde a beccaficu, sardines usually stuffed w/pine nuts &
raisins. A Sicilian specialty

sardella, fried baby fish minced w/olive oil & powdered
peppers from Calabria

sardina, small sardine

sardo, hard, aromatic cheese

sardoncini, little sardines

sartù, baked rice dish w/tomatoes, meatballs & mushrooms

savarin, cake baked in a ring mold & soaked in liquor. The
center is filled w/fruit & whipped cream

sbrisolona, flour, cornmeal & almond cake (crumble cake)

scalogno (i), shallot

scaloppa, veal scallop (thin slices of veal)

scaloppa alla fiorentina, veal scallop w/spinach & white sauce

scaloppa milanese, breaded, fried veal scallop

scaloppa napoletana, veal scallop coated in breadcrumbs

scaloppina (e), veal scallop

scaloppine alla boscaiola, veal scallops sautéed in oil & butter
& served w/an herb, black olive & onion sauce

scaloppine alla campagnola, veal scallops served in a sauce.
The term means "rustic"

scaloppine al marsala, small veal scallops in marsala wine

scaloppine al vino bianco, small veal scallops in
white-wine sauce

scamorza, mild cheese (aged *mozzarella*)

scampi, shrimp/prawns

scampi all'Americana, shrimp in a tomato sauce

scanello, sirloin

scapece, fried fish in vinegar & saffron/fried vegetables which
are then marinated

scarda, bream (fish)

scarola, escarole (a crispy leaf lettuce)

scarpaccia, zucchini pie (means "old shoe")

scarpena, scorpion fish

scelta, of your choice

schiacciata, flat bread (means "squashed flat")

schila, shrimp in Venice

schmarren, crêpes w/fruit & cream from Trentino-Alto Adige

scialatielli, wide noodles

scialcione, bread loaf

sciroppato (a), cooked in syrup

sciroppo, syrup

sciroppo d'acero, maple syrup

scodella, bowl

scorfano, scorpion fish

scorfano rosso, scorpion fish

scodella.

scorze d'amelle, pasta shaped like slivered almonds found in Basilicata

scorzonera, salsify

scotch, scotch

scottadito, grilled lamb chops

scottiglia di cinghiale, wild-boar chops

scrippelle, omelettes cut into thin strips & served in a meat broth. A specialty in Abruzzo & Molise

sebadas, bread filled w/cheese & honey, then fried. A Sardinian specialty

secco (a), dry. *Funghi secchi* are dried mushrooms

secondo piatto, second course

sedani, the name for a small pasta similar to *rigatoni*

sedano, celery

sedano rapa, celery root

segale, rye

sella, saddle

selvaggina, game/venison

semente/semenza/senze, seeds

semi di, seeds of...

semi di melone, pasta noodle for soup in the shape of melon seeds

semifreddi, (half-cold) desserts frozen or refrigerated before service

semigreggio integrale, semi-whole wheat rice

semolino, flour

semplice, plain
senape, mustard
senza, without
seppia (e), cuttlefish/squid
seppioline, small cuttlefish/squid
serpentone, pastry stuffed w/chopped figs, apples & nuts
servizio, service/service charge
servizio compreso, service included
servizio incluso, service included
servizio non compreso, service not included
servizio non incluso, service not included
sesamo, sesame
sete, thirsty
sevàdas, Sardinian deep-fried pastries
sfilatino, bread loaf
sfogie, Venetian word for sole
sfoglia/sfogliatella/sfogliatelli, flaky-crusted shell-shaped
    pastry filled w/sweetened *ricotta* cheese
sfogliata, flaky pastry
sfogliata di crema, cream puff
sformato, souffle
sfratti, sweet walnut rolls (a Christmas dessert)
sgavecio, pickled fish
sgombro (i), mackerel
sidro, cider
sigarette, cigarettes
silvano, chocolate tart
Silvestro, herb & mint liqueur
smacafam, *polenta* dish w/*asiago*
    cheese & sausage

Smacafam means hunger killer

Soave, slightly dry white wine from Veneto
sodo/sode, hard boiled
soffritto, sautéed/stock (the base for soup or the sauce for
    pasta) often made w/pigs' organs. Can also refer to slightly
    fried or browned onions, carrots & celery, a base for many
    dishes
sogliola, sole   *Sogliola SO-LEE-OH-LA*
sogliola all'Arlecchino, sole served w/a cream sauce
sogliola alla mugnaia, sole sautéed w/lemon, butter & parsley
sogliola margherita, sole covered w/hollandaise sauce
soia, soy
sopa, soup

sopa cauda, soup w/bread & roast pigeon
soppressa, sausage
soppressata, sausage/sausage made from pig's head
sorbetto, sherbet/sorbet
sorbetto al calvados, sherbet flavored w/apple brandy
sorrentina, often refers to a tomato, basil & mozzarrella sauce
sottaceti, pickles
sottaceto, pickled
sottoaceti, pickled vegetables/pickles
sottofiletto, beef or veal loin
sott'olio, in olive oil
sottonoce, top round of veal
spaccatina, bread loaf
spaghetti, spaghetti (long, thin pasta)
spaghetti aglio e olio, spaghetti w/olive oil & garlic
spaghetti alla bolognese, spaghetti w/meat sauce
spaghetti alla carbonara, spaghetti w/cream, bacon,
    cheese & egg
spaghetti alla checca, spaghetti w/raw tomatoes, basil & garlic
spaghetti alla gricia, spaghetti w/onions, bacon, pepper &
    grated cheese
spaghetti all'amatriciana, w/tomato sauce, cheese & garlic
spaghetti alle vongole, spaghetti w/clam sauce
spaghetti al ragù, pasta w/meat & tomato sauce
spaghettini, thin spaghetti
spaghetti pomodoro e basilico, spaghetti w/tomatoes & basil
spalla, shoulder
spanocci, very large prawns
sparaci, asparagus in Venice
sparnocci, type of shrimp
specialità della casa, specialty of the house
specialità di questa regione, specialty of the region
specialità di questo ristorante, specialty of the restaurant
specialità locali, local specialties
specialità regionali, regional specialties/local dishes
speck, cured ham found in the Trentino-Alto Adige region
spelt, a hard wheat
speziato, spicy
spezie, spice
spezzatino, meat or poultry stew/little pieces
spezzato, a stew
spicchio (d'aglio), clove (of garlic)

*Sotto a ceti
means
under vinegar*

spiedini alla corsara flambe, grilled meat served "flaming"

spiedini di mare, pieces of grilled fish on a skewer

spiedino (i), any dish roasted on a skewer

spiedo, allo, on a spit

spiga di grano, ear of corn

spigola, sea bass/grouper

spinaci, spinach

spiza di grano, ear of corn

spremuta, fresh fruit drink

spugnola, morel mushroom

spumante, sparkling wine

spumone (i), ice cream w/candied fruit, nuts & whipped cream

spumoni al croccante, *spumoni* topped w/toasted, caramelized almonds

spuntatura, breast of...

spuntino, snack

stagionato (a), well aged

stagione (i), season (in season)

starna, a type of partridge

stecca di, bar of

stecchi fritti, fried kebabs

stecchino, toothpick/skewer

stellette/stelline, star-shaped pasta

stinchetti, marzipan cakes (in the shape of human bones)

Stinco actually means shin bone.

stinco, braised veal or pork shank. The most common version of this dish is *stinco di maiale al forno*, a whole pork shank oven-roasted w/wine, garlic & rosemary

stoccafisso, dried cod

storione, sturgeon

stracchino, a soft, creamy white cheese

stracciate, scrambled eggs

stracciatella, egg-drop soup. This can also refer to chocolate-chip ice cream

stracotto, beef stew w/pork sausage/ pot roast

strangolapreti, see *strozzapreti*

strangozze, see *stringozzi*

strapazzate, scrambled

strascinati, shell-shaped pasta

stravecchio, *parmesan* cheese aged at least three years

Strega, a strong herb liqueur

strigghie, red mullet in Sicily

stringozzi, a homemade pasta from Umbria

strisce, ribbon noodles

strozzapreti, dumplings or *gnocchi* w/meat sauce.

strudel, this famous pastry roll can be found in Trentino-Alto Adige

strutto, lard

stufatino, pot roast or stew

stufato, braised/stewed/stew

stuzzicadenti, toothpicks

stuzzichino (i), appetizer

succhi di frutta, sweetened fruit juice

succo, juice

succo di frutta, fruit juice

succu tunnu, dumpling soup

soufflé, soufflé

sugna, lard

sugna piccante, a spicy sauce made from pork fat (added to dishes in Basilicata)

sugo, sauce/gravy/juice

sugo, al, w/tomato sauce

suino, pork

suppli/suppli di riso, breaded & deep-fried rice balls usually filled w/ham & cheese

suprema di pollo in gelatina, chicken breast in aspic

suro, mackerel

susina (e), plum

tacchino, turkey

tagliata di manzo, grilled beef

tagliatelle, short ribbon noodles

taglierini, thin noodles

taglierini alla chitarra, a pasta dish featuring a sheet of pasta cut w/a cutter called a *"chitarra"* or guitar

tagliolini, very narrow, thin flat noodles

tajarin, egg noodles found in Piedmont & Valle d'Aosta

taleggio, cheese w/a mild, buttery flavor

taralli, biscuits made in the shape of a ring

tartara, alla, raw w/lemon sauce

tartaruga, turtle

[handwritten marginalia:] Strozzapreti means Priest stranglers. A gluttonous priest supposedly choked to death on one.

[handwritten marginalia:] Succu tunnu. Never had it but love the name.

[handwritten marginalia:] tacchino TA-KEE·NO

tartina (e), open-faced sandwich/tart.
  Tartine are often appetizers
tartufi di cioccolato, chocolate "truffles"
  (chocolate-coated ice cream)
tartufi di mare, small clams/cockles
tartufo (i), truffle (funghi that grows around tree trunks)
tartufo di gelato, ice cream w/chocolate sauce
tartufo nero, black truffle from Tuscany
tasse, taxes. Menus will often indicate if *tasse e servizio* (taxes
  & service) are included
tavola (o), table
tavola calda, snack bar/fast food
tavoletta di cioccolata, chocolate bar
tazza, cup
tè, tea
tè cinese, Chinese tea
tè d'India, Indian tea
tè freddo, iced tea 
tegamaccio, lake-fish stew from Umbria
tegame/tegamino, al, sautéed
teglia, alla, pan-fried
teglia di pesce spada, marinated swordfish dish
tellina (e), clam
teneroni, veal chops
terrina, tureen
testa, head. *Testa di vitello* is calf's head
testina, head
testuggine, turtle
tiedde, fish casserole from Apulia
tiella, any dish with baked layers of ingredients
tiella di agnello, roasted lamb dish
tiella di riso e cozze, mussels, rice & potato dish found in
  Apulia
tigelle, flat bread
timbale/timballo, meat & vegetable casserole w/layers of pasta
timo, thyme
tinca (tinche), tench (seafood)
tiramisù, spongecake soaked in
  espresso & brandy w/cream &
  chocolate. *Marsala* can also
  be used in this
  delicious dessert

[handwritten: TAZZA di té.]

[handwritten: I'll pass.]

[handwritten: Tira misu made its way to Italy from the U.S.]

tirolese, alla, usually means
  w/fried onion rings
tisana, herbal tea
tisana al cinorrode, rose-hip tea
tisana al tiglio, lime tea
tisana camomilla, camomile tea
tocco di funghi, mushroom sauce
toc de purcit, pork stew w/white wine from
  Friuli-Venezia Giulia
toma, sharp cheese
tomini, fresh cheese from Piedmont
tonarelli/tonarrelli/tonnarelli, thin string pasta
tondino, bread loaf
tonica, tonic water
tonnato, in a tuna sauce. Can also refer to a cold veal dish
tonnetto, small tuna
tonno, tuna
topinambur, artichoke
  (Jerusalem artichoke)
tordo (i), thrush (a bird)
torlo, yolk
torrone, nougat
torta (e), tort/cake/pie
torta al pesto, spinach & cheese pie/flat
  bread cooked over hot stones in Umbria
  & filled w/cheese, meat or greens
torta di frutta, fruit tart
torta di gelato, ice-cream cake
torta di mele, apple tart
torta di tagliatelle, egg-noodle cake — *yes please.*
torta di verdure, sweet vegetable pie
  (similar to American pumpkin pie)
torta gianduia, chocolate & nut cake
torta meringa, large meringue pie filled w/fruit & topped
  w/whipped cream
torta millefoglie, napoleon (layers of pastry filled w/ice cream
  or whipped cream & topped w/frosting)
torta Pasqualina, Easter puff-pastry cake
torta rustica, cornmeal-cake dessert
torta sbrisolona, flour, cornmeal & almond cake
  (crumble cake)
torta tarantina, potato pie

Torrone is immensely popular in Italy!

torta turchesca, rice-pudding tart from Venice

torta zuccotto, liquor-soaked sponge cake filled w/ice cream or whipped cream, chocolate & candied fruits

tortelli di zucca, pasta stuffed w/pumpkin

tortellini, filled pasta rings

tortello (i), small doughnut/fritter

tortellone (i), a larger *tortellini* pasta

tortiera, cake/pie

tortiglione, almond cakes

tortiglioni, tube-shaped pasta (larger than *cannelloni*)

tortina di marmellata, jam tart

tortini di riso, rice cakes

tortino, tart/cheese & vegetable tart similar to quiche

tortino di carciofi, dish of fried artichokes & eggs

toscana, alla, w/tomatoes & herbs

tostato (a), toasted

totano (i), squid

tournedos, small tenderloin steaks

tovaglia, table cloth

tovagliolo, napkin

Tovagliolo
TOV-A-LEE-OH-LO

tozzetti, hazelnut & almond biscuits (flavored w/anise)

tracina dragone, a fish named "dragon" after its dangerous spines

tramezzino, small sandwich

trancia/trancio, piece/slice

trattaliu, cooked lamb intestines. A specialty in Sardinia

trenette, long, flat, thin ribbon noodles

trifolati, sliced mushrooms cooked in butter, garlic & oil

trifolato, w/truffles

triglia (e), red mullet

triglia alla Livornese, red mullet cooked w/tomatoes, garlic & parsley

trigoli, water chestnuts

trippa (e), tripe

trippa alla fiorentina, braised tripe & minced beef w/tomato sauce & cheese

trippa alla milanese, tripe w/onions, carrots, tomatoes, beans & leeks

trippa alla romana, tripe in a tomato & vegetable sauce

You can put all the "ALLA"s you want on trippa and it's still TRIPE.

tritato (a), ground (as in ground beef)

trofie, pasta similar to *gnocchi*

trombetta da morto, a type of mushroom

trota (e), trout

trota alle mandorle, stuffed-trout dish

trota di ruscello, river trout

trota iridea, rainbow trout

trota salmonata, salmon trout

trota spaccata, trout split in two, dipped in batter & deep-fried

trotella, trout

tuaca, a mixture of brandy, citrus fruits & herbs

tubetti, *macaroni*

tubi, refers to all tubular pasta

tuorlo, yolk

tutto compreso, all included

ua, grapes in Venice

ubriaco, cooked in red wine

uccelletti/uccelli, small birds (of all kinds) usually spit-roasted

uccelletto, all', w/tomato sauce & sage. *Piselli all' uccelleto* are peas cooked in tomato sauce w/sage

uccelli scappati, pork, pork sausage &/or small-bird kebabs

ueta, raisin in Venice

uliva, olive

umido, in, stewed

uopa, sea bream

uova, eggs

uova affogate, poached eggs

uova affogate nel vino, eggs poached in wine

uova à la coque, soft-boiled eggs

uova albume, egg whites

uova al burro, eggs fried in butter

uova al guscio, soft-boiled eggs

uova alla campagnola, eggs w/diced vegetables & cheese

uova alla coque, boiled eggs

uova alla fiorentina, fried eggs served on spinach

uova all'americana, fried eggs (usually served w/bacon)

uova alla russa, similar to deviled eggs

uova all'occhio di bue, fried eggs

uova al tegame con formaggio, fried eggs w/cheese

uova barrotte, soft-boiled eggs

uova bollite, soft-boiled eggs

[Handwritten margin notes: "Trombetta da morto... This sounds ominous." / "Tubi or not tubi..." / "uovo. uova."]

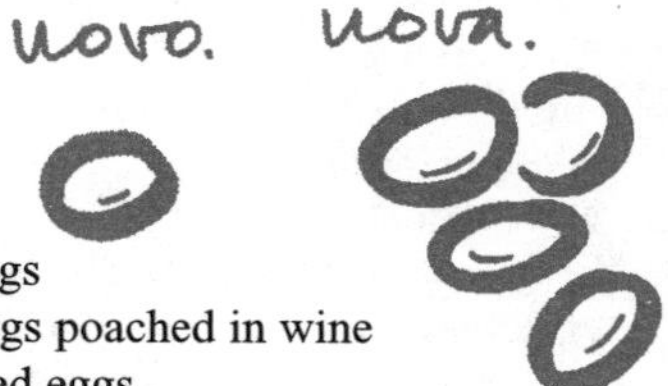

uova frittata/uova fritte, fried omelette
uova frittata al pomodoro, tomato omelette
uova frittata al prosciutto, ham omelette
uova in camicia, poached eggs
uova molli/uova mollette, soft-boiled eggs
uova ripiene, stuffed eggs
uova semplice, plain omelette
uova sode agli spinaci, eggs florentine
uova tonnate, hard-boiled eggs in tuna sauce
uovo (a), egg
uovo fritto (uova fritte), fried egg
uovo sodo (uova sode), hard-boiled egg
uovo strapazzato (uova strapazzate), scrambled egg
uva, grapes
uva bianca, green grapes
uva nera, black grapes
uva passa/uva passita, raisins
uva secca, raisin
uva spina, gooseberry
uvetta, white raisins
vaniglia, vanilla
valdostana, alla, usually means served w/ham & cheese
    (means "Valle d'Aosta style")
valigetta, roasted veal breast
Valpolicella, light (slightly bitter) red wine from Veneto
vapore, a, steamed
vario/vari, assorted
Vecchia Romagna, wine-distilled brandy
vegetable, vegetable
vegetariano (a), vegetarian
velluta, creamy soup
veneziana, alla, w/onions, white wine & sometimes mint
ventaglio, scallop
ventresca, white-meat tuna. Can also mean a boiled pork dish
verde, green/green pasta (w/a spinach base)
verde in pinzimonio, vegetable dip
Verdicchio, a dry white wine from Le Marche
verdura (e), green vegetable
verdura trovata, sautéed wild greens w/potatoes
verdure cotte, cooked vegetables
vermicelli, thin, long spaghetti noodles
vermut, vermouth

verza, cabbage
verzelata, grey mullet
vincigrassi/vincisgrassi, baked lasagna dish. Named after an
    Austrian prince, this dish is a specialty in the region of Le
    Marche where it is usually served w/chicken-giblet sauce
vincotto, a spread made from grapes
vinello, light wine
vino (i), wine
vino amabile, sweet wine
vino asciutto, very dry wine
vino bianco, white wine
vino brut, very dry wine
vino corposo, full-bodied wine
vino da pasto, table wine
vino da tavola, table wine
    (the lowest-quality wine made
    from any combination of grapes)

amabile also means loveable which pretty much refers to all wine as far as we're concerned.

vino del paese, local wine
vino dolce, sweet wine
vino frizzante, sparkling wine
vino leggero, light wine
vino nostrano, local wine
vino novello, new wine
vino rosatello, rosé wine
vino rosato, rosé wine
vino rosé, rosé (blush) wine
vino roseo, rosé wine
vino rosso, red wine

vino da tavola is low quality wine but not necessarily bad.

Vin Santo/Vinsanto, dessert wine from Tuscany & Trentino
vino secco, dry wine
vino semi secco, semi-sweet wine
vino spumante, sparkling wine
vino tipico, local wine
violino, cured leg of goat
visciola, wild cherry
vitellini, very young veal
vitello, veal
vitello all'uccelletto, diced veal & sage simmered in wine
vitello tonnato, cold veal w/tuna sauce
vodka, vodka
vol-au-vents, filled pastry shells
vongola (e), small clam

You weren't really looking this up were you?

vongole, alle, in a clam sauce
vongole oreganate, clams baked or broiled w/oregano
vongole veraci, small clams boiled in vinegar,
   hot pepper & garlic
whisky, whiskey
wurstel, hot dogs (similar to smoked hot dogs)
yogurt/yoghurt, yogurt
yogurt magro, low-calorie yogurt. *Yogurt intero* is not low-fat
zabaglione/zabaione, custard dessert flavored w/Marsala
zafferano, saffron
zalettini, shortbread cookies from Venice *I'll pass.*
zampa (e), pig's (or beef) feet
zampetto, pork leg
zampone, spicy sausage shaped like a pig's foot
zampone di maiale, stuffed pigs' feet
zelten, dried fruit & nut cake from Trentino-Alto Adige
zenzero, ginger
zèppola, doughnut/fritter *— Si, grazie!*
zesti, orange or lemon peel (can also be candied)
ziba, fragrant herb from Sardinia
zimini, in, cooked w/vegetables. *In zimino* can refer to spinach
   or Swiss chard stewed w/cod or squid & tomatoes
zimino, Sardinian fish stew
zingara, alla, "Gypsy style." Each chef has his or her own
   version of this sauce of many ingredients
zite (i), narrow, hollow-tube pasta
zucca, pumpkin or squash
zucca ovifera, squash
zucchero, sugar
zucchero a velo, powdered sugar
zucchero a zollette, lump sugar
zucchero greggio, brown sugar
zucchero grezzo, brown sugar
zucchero in pezzi, lump sugar
zucchero in polvere, powdered sugar   *Zucchine*   *ZOO·KEEN·E*
zucchine al burro versato, zucchini w/black-butter sauce
zucchine farcite, zucchini filled cheese, ham & mushrooms
zucchine fritte, deep-fried strips of zucchini
zucchine scapecce, pieces of zucchini fried in oil w/garlic
zucchine trifolate, sliced zucchini in butter, parsley & garlic
zucchino (i), zucchini
zucchio, zucchini

zuccotto, ice cream-filled cake
zuchette, zucchini
zuppa, soup
zuppa alla coltivatore, vegetable soup with diced bacon
zuppa alla pavese, soup w/croutons, grated cheese & poached egg
zuppa di arzilla, soup made w/ray fish & broccoli
zuppa di cereali, bean, vegetable & grain stew
zuppa di cipolle alla Francese, french onion soup
zuppa di cozze, mussel soup
zuppa di datteri, fish-soup specialty of Liguria
zuppa di farro, *spelt* (hard wheat) & bean soup
zuppa di frutti di mare, seafood soup
zuppa di pesce, fish stew
zuppa di pollo, chicken soup
zuppa di telline, soup w/tiny clams
zuppa di verdura, vegetable soup
zuppa di vongole, clam soup w/white wine
zuppa d'orzo, barley & potato soup
zuppa fredda, cold soup
zuppa inglese, not a soup at all. Spongecake soaked in liquor
  w/cream filling & whipped cream
zuppa pavese, clear soup w/a poached egg
zuppa valdostana, cabbage soup from the Val d'Aosta region

Zuppa di Farro... love it.

Buon Appetito!

Phone numbers, days closed and hours of operation often change, so it's advisable to check ahead. Restaurants in tourist areas may have different hours and days of operation during low season. Reservations are recommended for all restaurants unless noted. The telephone country code for Italy is 39.

Prices are for main courses and without wine. Lunch, even at the most expensive restaurants listed below, always has a lower fixed price. Credit cards are accepted unless noted otherwise.

Inexpensive: under $10
Moderate: $11 – $20
Expensive: $21 – $40
Very Expensive: over $40

We think, hope and pray that our restaurant list is current & correct, but remember... things change. Call first or do a "walk-by" in the afternoon. Stop in, make a reservation— they'll love you for it.

Alberobello
Trullo d'Oro
27 Via F. Cavallotti
080/4323909
Closed Sun. (dinner), Mon. and Jan.
Unique restaurant in *trulli* (limestone igloo-shaped houses) serving the cuisine of the region of Apulia.
Moderate

Amalfi
La Caravella
12 Via Matteo Camera
089/871029
Closed Tues. (in off season) and most of Nov. and Dec.
Family-run restaurant known for seafood dishes, especially *calamari* (squid) and *polpo* (octopus).
Moderate - Expensive

Da Gemma
9 Via Frà Gerardo Sasso
089/871345
Closed Wed. and mid-Jan. to mid-Feb.
Specialties of Campania (especially seafood) with summer dining on the terrace.
Moderate – Expensive

Aosta
Vecchia Aosta
4 Piazza Porta Pretoria
0165/361186
Closed Wed., part of Feb. and part of Nov.
Valdostan cuisine (including *fondue*) served in an interesting maze of dining areas between the inner and outer Roman walls.
Moderate

Ascoli Piceno
Ristorante Tornasacco
36 Piazza del Popolo
0736/254151
Closed Fri. and part of July.
Taste the specialties of Le Marche at this family-run restaurant.
Moderate

Assisi
La Fortezza
Vicolo della Fortezza (alley off of the Piazza del Comune)
075/812418
Closed Thurs. and Feb.
Traditional Umbrian dishes (including veal and rabbit).
Good food at a reasonable price.
Inexpensive – Moderate

Hotel Subasio (Ristorante)
2 Via Frate Elia
075/812206
Umbrian specialties in the shadow of the Basilica of St. Francis, with the best view in town from the dining terrace. A great place for a summer lunch.
Moderate

Bergamo
Taverna del Colleoni dell'Angelo
7 Piazza Vecchia
035/232596
Closed Mon. and part of Aug.
The specialties of Lombardy and the Lake District served
in a historic building in the heart of the old town.
Moderate – Expensive

Bologna
Anna Maria
17A Via Belle Arti
051/266894
Closed Mon., part of Jan. and part of Aug.
Try the homemade pasta in this popular *trattoria* near the
Opera House and the university. The *ragù* is excellent.
Moderate

Da Cesari
8 Via de'Carbonesi (south of Piazza Maggiore)
051/237710
Closed Sun., Sat. in July and most of Aug.
Romantic restaurant serving delicious Bolognese dishes
(try the veal Bolognese) along with homemade wine.
Moderate

Enoteca Italiana
2B Via Marsala (north of Piazza Maggiore)
051/235989
Closed Sun. and most of Aug.
Inexpensive deli and wine bar near the famous Neptune
Fountain.
Inexpensive

Bolzano
Zür Kaiserkron
1 Piazza della Mostra
0471/970770
Closed Sat. (dinner) and Sun.
Local dishes of Trentino-Alto Adige, in a historic building
near the Gothic cathedral. The food is Italian with an
Austrian influence.
Moderate – Expensive

Cagliari
Dal Corsaro
28 Viale Regina Margherita
070/664318
Closed Sun. and part of Aug.
Lively restaurant serving Sardinian specialties such as
porcheddu (roast suckling pig).
Moderate – Expensive

Capri
Da Gemma
6 Via Madre Serafina
081/8370461
Closed some Mon. and Nov. through March
Restaurant-pizzeria serving Caprese specialties (especially
seafood). Try the *fritto alla Gemma* (a mixture of fried
mozzarella, zucchini and vegetables).
Moderate

Castellina in Chianti
Le Tre Porte
4-6-8 Via Trento e Trieste
0577/741163
Closed Tues.
Friendly service at this unassuming restaurant and pizzeria
in a small Tuscan town. Try the *pappardelle sulla lepre*
(strips of pasta w/rabbit sauce).
Moderate

Cernobbio
Il Gatto Nero
69 Via Monte Santa
031/512042
Closed Closed Mon. and Tues. (lunch)
This restaurant overlooks Cernobbio and serves the specialties of the area surrounding Lake Como (especially fresh
fish). An excellent pine-nut *risotto* is often on the menu.
Moderate

Corniglia
Da Mananan
117 Via Fleschi
0187/821166
Closed Tues.
Hearty fare served in the cellar of a home in the smallest
Cinque Terre town. Many dishes feature *pesto*. Try the
pansoti (triangular-shaped filled pasta).
Moderate

Florence
All'Antico Vinaio
65R Via de'Neri (near the Palazza Vecchio)
055/282738
Closed Sun.
This tiny wine bar serves over 150 wines, *panini* (sandwiches) and local specialties such as *ribollita* (vegetable
soup thickened with bread).
Inexpensive – Moderate

Angiolino
36R Via Santo Spirito
055/2398976
Closed Mon.
Popular *trattoria* with stone walls, a large wooden stove in
the middle, and wrought-iron fixtures. Good pasta and
meat dishes at reasonable prices.
Inexpensive – Moderate

Benvenuto
16R Via Mosca (corner of Via Mosca and Via Neri)
055/214833
Closed Sun. and part of Aug.
Small *trattoria* serving Florentine specialties, and a
favorite of budget travelers.
Inexpensive – Moderate

Buca dell'Orafo
28R Via Volta dei Girolami
055/213619
Closed. Sun., Mon. and part of Aug.
No credit cards.

Tuscan specialties served in the cellar of a former gold-smith shop (*orafo*) near the Uffizi.
Inexpensive – Moderate

Buca Lapi
1R Via del Trebbio
055/213768
Closed Sun., Mon. (lunch) and part of Aug.
This restaurant is in a cellar located under the Palazzo Antinori. Try the *scampi giganti alla griglia* under the vaulted ceiling, surrounded by old travel posters.
Moderate – Expensive

Cantinetta Antinori
3 Piazza Antinori
055/292234
Closed weekends and Aug.
Tuscan cuisine served in a *palazzo* and known for its wine list. Both a restaurant and wine bar.
Moderate – Expensive

La Carabaccia
190R Via Palazzuolo
055/214782
Closed Sun. and Mon. (lunch)
Florentine cuisine at reasonable prices. The specialty here is *zuppa carabaccia* (creamy onion soup served w/croutons).
Moderate

Il Cibreo
8R Via Verrochio (near Via di San Giuseppe)
055/2341100
Closed Sun., Mon. and Aug.
Florentine cuisine at this attractive and popular restaurant, café and *trattoria*. Try the *sformato* (souffle). The *trattoria* (Cibreino) does not take reservations.
Moderate (in the *trattoria*) – Expensive (restaurant)

Don Chisciotte
4R Via Ridolfi (in the area near Piazza Santa Maria Novella)
055/475430
Closed Sun., Mon (lunch) and part of Aug.
Tuscan restaurant specializing in seafood and known for its
innovative *risotto* dishes.
Expensive

Corsini
4 Lungarno Corsini (near Ponte Vecchio)
055/244285
Closed Mon.
International crowd, elegant setting in a former palace and
Florentine cuisine all combine for a memorable evening.
Expensive

Trattoria Le Mossacce
55R Via del Pronconsolo (near Piazza del Duomo)
055/294361
Closed Sat., Sun. and Aug. No reservations
Dine with locals on Florentine cuisine at reasonable prices,
including *ossobuco* (braised veal shank). The restaurant has
been around since the early 1900s.
Inexpensive – Moderate

Vivoli
7R Via Isola delle Stinche (a backstreet near Santa Croce)
055/292334
Closed Mon. and Aug.
The best ice-cream shop (*gelateria*) in Italy.
Inexpensive

Genoa
Da Genio
61R Salita San Leonardo (near Piazza Dante)
010/588463
Closed Sun. and Aug.
Traditional *trattoria* serving Genovese dishes such as *trenette al
pesto* (long, flat, thin ribbon noodles with pesto).
Inexpensive – Moderate

Zeffirino
20 Via XX Settembre
010/591990
Open daily. Jacket and tie required
Family-run restaurant since the 1930s. Ligurian specialties
such as *frittura del golfa* (mixed fried seafood from the Gulf
of Genoa) are served here, and there is a huge wine list.
Expensive

L'Aquila
Elodia
17B del Gran Sasso
0862/606219
Closed Sun. (dinner) and Mon.
Local specialties of Abruzzo and Molise in the capital
of Abruzzo. You won't find many North American
travelers here. Montepulciano d'Abruzzo wine is a favorite.
Moderate

Lerici
Conchiglia
3Piazza del Molo
0187/967334
Closed Wed. (except in high tourist season)
Seafront *trattoria* specializing in fresh seafood.
Moderate

Locarno, Switzerland
Ristorante Zurigo
9 Viale Verbano
41(country code)/091/7431617
Open daily
Located in a Mediterranean-style hotel, this restaurant
serves Italian and Swiss specialties in its dining room and
on the lovely terrace. Try the *saltimbocca*!
Moderate – Expensive

Lucca
Giglio
2 Piazza del Giglio
0583/494058
Closed Tues. (dinner), Wed., part of Feb. and part of July.
A small *trattoria* known for seafood dishes. The homemade
tortellini is delicious.
Moderate

Da Giulio
45 Via delle Conce (Piazza San Donato)
0583/55948
Closed Mon. and some Sun.
Locals dine here on Tuscan specialties. Located near the city
walls. No frills here, just hearty food.
Inexpensive – Moderate

Lugano, Switzerland
La Tinera
2 Via dei Gorini
41(country code)/091/9235219
Closed Sun. and Aug.
Small cellar *trattoria* serving Ticino specialties in the center of this
historic town. Regional wine is served in traditional ceramic bowls.
Inexpensive – Moderate

Mantua (Mantova)
L'Aquila Nigra
4 Vicolo Bonacolsi
0376/327180
Closed most Sun., Mon. and part of Aug.
Elegant dining (featuring the cuisine of Lombardy) in a 15th-
century *palazzo*.
Moderate – Expensive

Matera
Oi Marì
66 Vico Fiorentini
0835/346121
Closed Tues.
Basilicata cuisine served in a restored caves. Great pizza!
Inexpensive

Milan

Bagutta
14 Via Bagutta
02/76002767
Closed Sun. and Aug.
Popular *trattoria* serving specialties of Lombardy. There's a huge *antipasto* table. We always have a great time here.
Moderate

Biffi
In the Galleria Vittorio Emmanuele
02/8057961
A bar and restaurant that's a great place for a snack, lunch or a drink. You can either eat in the restaurant or, for some interesting people-watching, at tables in the Galleria.
Moderate

Boeucc
2 Piazza Belgioioso
02/76020224
Closed Sat., Sun. (lunch) and Aug.
Milan's oldest restaurant in an elegant setting near the Duomo.
Expensive

Peck
4 Via Victor Hugo
02/876774 (restaurant)/02/861040 (wine bar)
Closed Sun. and part of July
Restaurant, delicatessen, cafeteria, take-out counter and wine bar (Bottega del Vino) all at this gourmet food store.
Expensive – Moderate – Inexpensive

Savini
Galleria Vittorio Emanuele II
02/72003433
Closed Sun. and part of Aug.
The best of Lombardy served in the famous and beautiful Galleria.
Expensive – Very Expensive

Monterosso
Miky
104 Via Fegina (Monterosso al Mare)
0187/817608
Open daily
Ligurian seafood served in this charming Cinque Terre town.
Moderate

Naples
Brandi
1 Salita San Anna di Palazzo (off of Via Chiaia)
081/416928
Closed Mon. and part of Aug.
Many places claim to have made the first pizza, but it is likely
that the first *pizza margherita* was made here.
Inexpensive

Mimì alla Ferrovia
21 Via Alfonso d'Aragona
081/5538525
Closed Sun. and part of Aug.
Local favorite for classic Neapolitan cuisine. Try the *linguine
alla Mimì* (flat noodles with a shrimp sauce).
Moderate

La Sacrestia
116 Via Orazio
081/664186
Closed Sun. (dinner) and part of Aug.
Hard to find in the maze of streets above the port, this restaurant provides a view of the harbor in good weather, but you
really come here for the Neapolitan specialties.
Moderate –Expensive

Orta San Giulio
Olina
40 Via Olina
0322/905656
Closed Wed.
Small restaurant/hotel in the center of this picturesque town on
Lake Orta serving the specialties of the Lake District.
Moderate

Orvieto
Le Grotte del Funaro
41 Via Ripa Serancia
0763/343276
Closed Mon.
Umbrian specialties served in a *grotte* (cave).
Inexpensive – Moderate

Palermo
Antica Focacceria San Francesco
58 Via Paternostro (Mercado Vucciria)
091/320264
Closed Tues. No credit cards
Stuffed *focaccia* sandwiches and Sicilian snacks at this neighborhood bakery in the heart of the old town. In business since 1834, you'll feel like you stepped back in time.
Inexpensive

Perugia
Il Falchetto
20 Via Bartolo
075/5731775
Closed Mon. and part of Jan.
Umbrian specialties in medieval dining rooms.
Moderate – Expensive

La Taverna
8 Via delle Streghe (off Corso Vannucci)
075/5724128
Closed Mon.
Traditional Umbrian food in the heart of the historic center. Attentive service in a medieval house.
Moderate

Pisa
Bruno
12 Via Luigi Bianchi
050/560818
Closed Mon. (dinner) and Tues.
Classic Tuscan food near the Leaning Tower. Try the *zuppa alla paesana* (thick vegetable soup).
Moderate

Portofino
Il Pitosforo
8-9 Via Molo Umberto I
0185/269020
Closed Mon., Tues. and some winter months.
Famous and expensive, this harborside restaurant serves
Ligurian specialties.
Expensive – Very Expensive

Positano
Buca di Bacco
8 Via Rampa Teglia
089/875699
Closed Nov. - March
Specialties of Campania at this seaside restaurant and café. The
speciality here is *zuppa di cozze* (mussel soup).
Expensive

Ravenna
Bella Venezia
16 Via IV Novembre
0544/212746
Closed Sun. and part of Jan.
Family-run restaurant near the Piazza del Popolo serving home-
made pasta and other specialties of Emilia-Romagna.
Moderate

Rome
Abruzzi
1 Via del Vaccaro (off Piazza Santi Apostoli near Piazza
Venezia)
06/6793897
Closed Sat. and part of Aug.
Taste the specialties of the Abruzzo region at this simple *tratto-
ria*. Try the Abruzzi pasta dishes, especially the *cannelloni*.
Inexpensive

Al 34 (Il Ristorante 34)
34 Via Mario de'Fiori (near the Spanish Steps)
06/6795091
Closed Mon. and Aug.
Good food featuring Roman specialties at this affordable,

romantic (candlelit) and popular *trattoria*. Try the *tagliata di manzo* (grilled beef).
Moderate – Expensive

Antico Arco
7 Piazzale Aurelio
06/5815274
Closed Sun. and part of Aug.
Attentive service, a modern setting and fine Roman food make this a popular place. Delicious chocolate desserts. It's a little out of the way at the top of Janiculum Hill.
Moderate

Antico Caffé della Pace
3 Via della Pace (near Piazza Navona)
06/6861216
Attractive cafe with indoor and outdoor seating. Great place for a relaxing drink and snack near the Church of Santa Maria della Pace.
Inexpensive

Arancia Blu
55-65 Via dei Latini (at Via Arunci)
06/4454105
No credit cards. No lunch
Inventive vegetarian cuisine (and vegan dishes upon request) at this interesting restaurant in the San Lorenzo area (a neighborhood in transition). Try one of the *ravioli ripieni* (stuffed ravioli) dishes. The good news for vegetarians is that most restaurants offer pasta dishes without meat.
Moderate

Il Bacaro
27 Via degli Spagnoli
06/6864110
Closed Sun.
Small, unpretentious restaurant on a small alley near the Piazza delle Copelle (a huge ivy covers the entrance). Delicious *risotto*.
Moderate

Bistro
40 Via Palestro (near the Termini train station)
06/44702868
Closed Sun. (lunch)
Beautiful bistro and wine bar serving interesting dishes
such as *taglionini* with lobster (made blue-green with
curaçao liqueur). Huge wine list.
Moderate – Expensive

La Campana
18 Vicolo della Campana
06/6867820
Closed Mon. and Aug.
Simple Roman fare near the intersection of Via Font.
Borghese and Via della Scrofa near the Piazza Navona. It's
said to be the oldest eatery in Rome.
Moderate

La Carbonara
23 Piazza Campo dei Fiori
06/6864783
Closed Tues. and part of Aug.
Trattoria serving Roman cuisine including *carbonara*
(hence the restaurant name). On Piazza Campo dei Fiori.
Moderate

La Cisterna
13 Via della Cisterna
06/5812543
Closed Sun.
Regional favorites of the Lazio region served in a family-
run restaurant in Trastevere. Try the grilled *gamberi*.
Moderate

Dal Bolognese
1-2 Piazza del Popolo
06/3611426
Closed Mon. and part of Aug.
Bolognese cuisine served on the Piazza del Popolo. Top off
your dinner with a *digestivo* (after-dinner drink) and
dessert at Rosati, the fashionable cafe next door.
Moderate – Expensive

Enoteca Corsi
89 Via del Gesú (off of Via del Plebescito)
06/6790821
Closed Sun. and Aug.
Wine bar serving Roman cuisine at common-seating tables
in a 1937 storefront. An inexpensive choice for lunch.
Inexpensive

'Gusto
9 Piazza Augusto Imperatore (near Via del Corso)
06/3226273
Open daily
Something for every food lover! A *pizzeria*, wine bar,
cookware shop and restaurant. Always crowded.
Moderate

Hostaria Giulio
19 Via della Barchetta (near Via dei Monserrato)
06/68806466
Closed Sun.
Friendly service and Roman specialties (especially fish and
pasta) at this *hostaria* with outdoor seating.
Moderate

I Leoni d'Abruzzo
44 Via Vicenza (near the Termini train station)
06/44700272
Closed Sun., Aug. and some winter months
Good food and pleasant service at this (a little too brightly
lit) restaurant, where the *menu del giorno* (the menu of the
day) appeals to both locals and hotel guests alike. Forget
the tourist menu and use this guide to decipher the more
interesting local fare.
Inexpensive – Moderate

Da Luigi
24 Piazza Sforza Cesarini (off of Corso Vittorio Emanuele
not too far from Piazza Navona)
06/6865946
Outdoor and indoor dining at this *trattoria* on the charming
Piazza Sforza Cesarini. Try the *penne alla vodka*.
Moderate

Orso "80"
33 Via dell'Orso (a short distance north and west of Piazza Navona)
06/6864904
Closed Mon. and Aug.
This restaurant is known for its *antipasto* table as well as its pasta dishes. Crowded and popular with tourists.
Moderate

Osteria Mia
13 Vicolo della Cancelleria (off of Corso Vittorio Emanuele not too far from Piazza Navona)
06/68892729
Friendly *osteria* with a brick-vaulted ceiling and delicious pasta dishes. The house wine is less than 10 euros a bottle- and delicious.
Moderate

Polese
40 Piazza Sforza Cesarini
06/6861709
Another restaurant on the Piazza Sforza Cesarini (see Da Luigi above) where you can eat inexpensively. Try the *fettuccine alla Polese* (fettuccine w/cream and mushrooms).
Inexpensive – Moderate

Porto di Ripetta
250 Via di Ripetta
06/3612376
Closed Sun.
Dine on Mediterranean cuisine under an attractive brick-vaulted ceiling at this restaurant a few blocks from the Piazza del Popolo.
Moderate

Rosetta
8 Via della Rosetta
06/6861002
Closed Sat. (lunch), Sun. and part of Aug.
Located near Piazza della Rotonda and the Pantheon, and known for its seafood. There is no meat on the menu.
Very Expensive

Sabatini
13 Piazza Santa Maria in Trastevere
06/5812026
Closed part of Aug.
Lively and popular restaurant in Trastevere serving Roman
cuisine (especially seafood). The restaurant faces the
Church of Santa Maria in Trastevere. Known for its
spaghetti alle vongole (spaghetti in a white clam sauce).
Expensive

La Terrazza
49 Via Ludovisi
06/478121
This very expensive and formal restaurant in the Hotel
Eden (several blocks off the Via Veneto) offers memorable
food and a view of St. Peter's.
Very Expensive

Vecchia Roma
18 Piazza Campitelli
06/6864604
Closed Wed. and part of Aug.
A great place to dine outdoors in the summer months, this
trattoria serves classic Roman fare in the Jewish Ghetto
area. Delicious *risotto* dishes.
Moderate

Rome: Food and Wine Stores

Buccone
19 Via di Ripetta (near the Piazza del Popolo)
06/3612154
This wine bar is a great place for lunch. You can also buy
wines from every region of Italy.
Inexpensive

Castroni
196 Via Cola di Rienzo
06/6874383
A food market where you can buy specialties from every
region of Italy.

Confetteria Moriondo & Gariglio
21-22 Pie di Marmo
Small *confetteria* (candy shop). The chocolates are made on the premises, and the smells are wonderful.

Enoteca al Parlamento di Achilli
15 Via de' Prefetti
06/6873446
Wine bar and food shop with a large selection of *grappas* and pickled foods.

Enoteca di Sardena
3 Via della Pigna
06/6789374
Tiny shop devoted solely to wine, liqueur, cheese, sweets, pasta and meat from the island of Sardinia.

Ai Monasteri
72 Corso Rinascimento (near Piazza Navona)
06/68802783
Wine, liquor, chocolates and other food items produced by Italian religious orders.

Trimani
20 Via Grotto
06/4469661
180-year-old store/bar with over 5000 wines, liqueurs and *grappas*. Over 50 wines by the glass available at the bar.

Rome: Food Markets

Campo dei Fiori
6 a.m. – noon
Mon. – Sat.

Piazza Vittorio Emanuele
7 a.m. – noon
Mon. – Sat.

San Gimignano
Bel Soggiorno
91 Via San Giovanni
0577/940375
Closed Wed.
Tuscan specialties served in a 100-year-old hotel located in this beautiful walled town. Lots of game dishes on the menu.
Moderate

Siena
Le Logge
33 Via del Porrione
0577/48013
Closed Sun. and part of Jan.
Tuscan dishes at this *osteria* near the Piazza del Campo (one of Italy's most beautiful squares).
Moderate

Enoteca Italica
Fortezza Medicea/Viale Maccari
0577/288497
Closed Sun.
The Italian government operates this "Library of Wine" where you can taste wines from every region of Italy.
Inexpensive

Spoleto
Il Tartufo
24 Piazza Garibadli (near the amphitheater)
0743/40236
Closed Sun. (dinner), Mon., part of Jan. and part of July
Spoleto's oldest restaurant has a rustic first floor and modern second floor. Many dishes (especially the more expensive ones) feature *tartufi* (truffles).
Moderate

Taormina
Luraleo
27 Bagnoli Croce
0942/24279
Closed Wed. in winter.
Indoor and outdoor dining at this restaurant specializing in
Sicilian dishes (especially grilled fish).
Moderate

Trieste
Harry's Grill
2 Piazza Unità d'Italia
040/660606
This restaurant (located in the Grand Hotel Duchi
d'Aosta) serves international fare, which is appropriate
considering the Italian, Austrian and Slavic influences
found here.
Moderate – Expensive

Trieste (San Giovanni)
Suban
2 Via Emilio Comici
040/54368
Closed Mon. (lunch), Tues. and part of Aug.
In the hills two miles north of Trieste, this *trattoria* serves
specialties of the Friuli-Venezia Giulia region.
Moderate

Turin
Da Mauro
21 Via Maria Vittoria
011/8170604
Closed Mon. and July
Family-run *trattoria* near the Piazza San Carlo serving
Piedmontese and Tuscan dishes. Delicious *cannelloni*.
Inexpensive

Vintage 1997
16 Piazza Solferino
011/535948
Closed Sat. (lunch), Sun., and part of Aug.

Popular restaurant where you should try the Piedmontese tasting menu when available.
Moderate – Expensive

Venice
Avogaria
1629 Calle della Avogaria (near Ponte San Sebastian)
041/2960491
San Basilio vaporetto
Modern, minimalist decor and southern Italian cuisine make this restaurant stand out in the Dorsoduro.
Moderate

Da Arturo
3656A Calle degli Assassini
Rialto vaporetto. Between Campo San Angelo and Campo Manin.
041/5286974
Closed Sun. and Aug.
No credit cards.
No seafood at this tiny, popular restaurant. Try the pasta *gorgonzola*.
Moderate

Cavatappi
525 Campo della Guerra (behind Piazza San Marco)
Vallaresso vaporetto
041/2960252
Closed Sun. in winter and Jan.
Small wine bar (the name means "corkscrew") where you can sample wine, light meals and *cicheti* (bite-sized snacks).
Moderate

Al Covo
3968 Campiello della Pescaria
Riva Degli Schiavoni vaporetto. Located off of Riva degli Schiavoni.
041/5223812
Closed Wed., Thurs. and part of Aug.
No credit cards.
Fresh Venetian specialties (especially seafood) at this small *osteria*.
Moderate – Expensive

Da Franz
754 Fondamenta San Isepo
Giardini vaporetto. Near the Biennale Gardens.
041/5220861
Hostaria serving Venetian specialties. The food is great,
but you might need help from the hotel staff to get there.
It's worth the trip.
Expensive

Ai Gondolier
366 Fondamenta de l'Ospedaleto
Santa Maria Della Salute vaporetto. Located near the
Guggenheim Museum.
041/5286396
Closed Tues.
Not for seafood lovers. This restaurant serves meat dishes.
Delicious *fiori di zucca* (zucchini flowers filled w/cheese,
battered and fried).
Moderate – Expensive

Harry's Bar
1323 Calle Vallaresso
San Marco vaporetto.
041/5285777
Famous restaurant serving Venetian specialties. The food is
very expensive and we have heard many complaints, so you
may just want to have a martini or a *Bellini* (peach juice and
Prosecco) at the bar.
Very Expensive

Da Ivo
1809 Calle dei Fuseri
San Marco vaporetto. Located near Campo S. Luca.
041/5285004
Closed Sun. and Jan.
Comfortable and beautiful restaurant serving Venetian (and
Tuscan) specialties. It's known for its delicious and filling
bistecca alla Fiorentina (T-bone steak).
Expensive

Al Mascaron
5225 Calle Longa Santa Maria Formosa
Rialto vaporetto
041/5225995
Closed Sun.
No credit cards.
You might have to sit next to strangers at long tables in
this unpretentious restaurant/bar. The food is straightfor-
ward Venetian. Try the deep-fried *calamari*.
Moderate

Il Refolo
1459 Campiello del Piovan (Campo San Giacomo
dell'Orio)
Riva di Biasio or San Stae vaporetto
041/5240016
Closed Mon. and Dec. through Feb.
This pizzeria/restaurant is on a picturesque square overlooking the church of San Giacomo dell'Orio. Customers
dock their boats along the patio for take-out.
Moderate

Da Remigio
Salizzada dei Greci
Riva del Schiavoni or San Zaccaria vaporetto
041/5230089
Closed Mon. (dinner) and Tues.
Small, family-style Venetian *trattoria* serving seafood (usu-
ally grilled and sold by weight), pasta and meat dishes.
Moderate

Taverna La Fenice
1939 Campiello de la Fenice
San Marco vaporetto
041/5223856
Closed Sun. (except in summer).
Elegant Venetian dining (indoors and outdoors). Try the
tagliatelle with cream sauce.
Moderate – Expensive

Trattoria alla Madonna
594 Calle della Madonna
Rialto vaporetto
041/5223824
Closed Wed., Jan. and part of Aug.
Near the Rialto, this *trattoria* specializes in fresh grilled fish.
You will also find pasta and meat dishes, and Venetian specialties such as *fegato alla veneziana* (liver and onions).
Inexpensive – Moderate

Vini da Gigio
3628A Fondamenta San Felice
Cá d'Oro vaporetto
041/5285140
Closed Mon., part of Jan. and part of Aug.
Wine bar and *osteria* serving Venetian specialties. A little off
the beaten track, just off the Strada Nuova.
Moderate

Vino Vino
2007A Ponte delle Veste
S. M. del Giglio vaporetto. Located near Campo S. Angelo
and Campo S. Fantin.
041/2417688
Closed Tues.
Popular wine bar and restaurant serving typical Venetian cuisine.
Inexpensive – Moderate

Vernazza
Gambero Rosso
7 Piazza Marconi
0187/812265
Closed Mon. and from Nov. – Feb.
Ligurian specialties at this Cinque Terre restaurant (it's been
open for over 100 years) located on the harbor.
Moderate

Restaurants by Location

Descriptions of restaurants in the cities listed here can be found on the page number following each city.

THINGS CHANGE!

Phone numbers, prices, addresses, quality of food, etc., all change. If you come across any new information, we'd appreciate hearing from you. No item is too small! Drop us an e-mail note at:

www.eatndrink.com

Books in this series are available in bulk purchases at special discounts for promotions or premiums. Special editions, including corporate imprints and personalized covers, can be created in large quantities. For more information, contact the publisher or authors.

ACKNOWLEDGMENTS

Thanks to Doug Morris, the author of Open Road Publishing's Italy Guide, for all of his suggestions and help with this book. His insight into Italy is incredible, and he proved to be an invaluable resource. Thanks also to Jonathan Stein, our Open Road publisher.

Marian Olson (our Miss Know-It-All English editor) and Angelina Bellotti Scharlau (our Italian editor) were of great help in the original edition of this book and in this second edition.

Special thanks to those who have helped us find the restaurants in this guide, especially Mark Berry and Dan Schmidt who suffered through many meals and countless bottles of wine on our behalf.

RESTAURANT AND FOOD NOTES